AUGSBURG TODAY: THIS WE BELIEVE, TEACH AND CONFESS

Edited by David L. Mahsman

CONCORDIA PUBLISHING HOUSE • SAINT LOUIS

Project editor: Kenneth Wagener

Unless otherwise noted, Scripture quotations are taken from the HOLY BIBLE, NEW INTERNATIONAL VERSION®. NIV®. Copyright © 1973, 1978, 1984 by the International Bible Society. Used by permission of Zondervan Publishing House. All rights reserved.

Scripture quotations marked KJV are from the King James or Authorized Version of the Bible.

Scripture quotations marked NRSV are from the New Revised Standard Version, Copyright © 1989 Division of Christian Education of the National Council of the Churches of Christ in the United States of America, and are used by permission. All rights reserved.

The Augsburg Confession is reprinted from *The Book of Concord,* edited by Theodore G. Tappert, Copyright © 1959 Fortress Press. Used by permission of Augsburg Fortress.

Copyright © 1997 Concordia Publishing House
3558 S. Jefferson Avenue, St. Louis, MO 63118-3968
Manufactured in the United States of America

All rights reserved. No part of this publication may be reproduced, stored in a retrieval system, or transmitted, in any form or by any means, electronic, mechanical, photocopying, recording, or otherwise, without the prior written permission of Concordia Publishing House.

CONTENTS

List of Authors 4

Abbreviations 5

Introduction 6

The Augsburg Confession 8

God/Creation (Article 1) 19

Sin [Original Sin] (Articles 2 and 19) 25

Jesus Christ [Son of God] (Article 3) 31

Justification (Article 4) 36

Means of Grace [Office of the Ministry] (Article 5) 42

New Obedience (Articles 6 and 20) 46

Church (Articles 7 and 8) 51

Baptism (Article 9) 56

Lord's Supper (Article 10) 61

Confession/Absolution *and* Repentance (Articles 11 and 12) 66

Use of the Sacraments (Article 13) 71

Order in the Church [Ministry] (Article 14) 75

Church Usages [Traditions] (Article 15) 82

Civil Government [Christians and Government] (Article 16) 88

Return of Christ (Article 17) 93

Freedom of the Will (Article 18) 99

The One Mediator [Cult of Saints] (Article 21) 103

Answers and Comments 108

LIST OF AUTHORS

Dr. Charles P. Arand is assistant professor of systematic theology at Concordia Seminary, St. Louis.

Dr. Jerald C. Joersz is assistant executive director of The Lutheran Church—Missouri Synod's Commission on Theology and Church Relations.

Dr. Richard G. Kapfer is president of the Iowa District West of The Lutheran Church—Missouri Synod and chairman of the LCMS Commission on Theology and Church Relations.

Dr. Eugene F. Klug is professor emeritus of systematic theology at Concordia Theological Seminary, Fort Wayne, Ind.

The Rev. Joel Lehenbauer is assistant executive director of the LCMS Commission on Theology and Church Relations.

The Rev. David Liefeld chairs the Washington Advisory Council for the LCMS Office of Government Information.

Dr. Gregory Lockwood is associate professor of exegetical theology at Concordia Theological Seminary, Fort Wayne, Ind.

Dr. David A. Lumpp is associate professor of religion at Concordia College, St. Paul, Minn.

The Rev. David L. Mahsman is executive editor of *The Lutheran Witness* magazine.

Dr. Thomas Manteufel is associate professor of systematic theology at Concordia Seminary, St. Louis.

Dr. Samuel H. Nafzger is executive director of the LCMS Commission on Theology and Church Relations.

The Rev. John T. Pless is pastor of University Lutheran Chapel in Minneapolis.

Dr. J.A.O. Preus III is associate professor of systematic theology and dean of faculty at Concordia Seminary, St. Louis.

Dr. Francis C. Rossow is professor of practical theology at Concordia Seminary, St. Louis.

Dr. David P. Scaer is professor of systematic theology at Concordia Theological Seminary, Fort Wayne, Ind.

The questions, "For Reflection," were written by Rev. Roger Gallup, Bethlehem Lutheran Church, River Grove, Ill.; Rev. Steven Cornwell, Concordia, Hillside, and St. John, Bellwood, Ill.; Rev. Dr. Martin Noland, Christ Lutheran Church, Oak Park, Ill.; Rev. David Fleming, Our Savior, Grand Rapids, Mich.

ABBREVIATIONS

AC—Augsburg Confession
Ap—Apology of the Augsburg Confession
FC—Formula of Concord
LC—Large Catechism
SA—Smalcald Articles
SC—Small Catechism
SD—Solid Declaration of the Formula of Concord
Tr—Treatise on the Power and Primacy of the Pope

Numerals following the above abbreviations denote article numbers, except in the Smalcald Articles, where they refer to parts. In the Smalcald Articles, article numbers follow the comma after the part numbers. In all other cases, the numeral following the comma identifies the paragraph(s) from which the citation is taken.

INTRODUCTION

David L. Mahsman

"Whether it's middle age or the coming millennium or a bad case of the blues, many Americans are on a quest for spiritual meaning."
Newsweek, Nov. 28, 1994.

The "new" quest for spiritual satisfaction ought come as no surprise. Human beings are innately religious. God made us that way.

But where are seekers looking for spiritual satisfaction? Some, of course, look to Christianity in one form or another. Some explore religions of other cultures. Others wade into the New Age, goddess worship or seminars that present the concoctions of entrepreneurs who know an opportunity when they see one. Many seekers pick and choose beliefs and practices, cafeteria-style, to cook up a very personal religion.

While our American culture would have us believe that one person's spiritual notions are just as valid as another's, the apostle John takes a different tack: "Dear friends, do not believe every spirit, but test the spirits to see whether they are from God, because many false prophets have gone out into the world" (1 John 4:1).

Left to our own devices, we are easily deceived. Left to our own devices, we can have no certainty about things spiritual.

But God does not leave us to our own devices. Rather, He has revealed Himself to us. Through Holy Scripture, He tells us about Himself and about ourselves. Jesus proclaimed in prayer to His heavenly Father, "Your word is truth" (John 17:17).

Because God's Word is the only reliable and trustworthy source of spiritual truth, Lutherans historically have insisted that Christian teaching be derived only from Holy Scripture. It is not to be based, even in part, on human speculation or logic, on church tradition, or on personal feelings or experience. Thus the Reformation-era slogan, *Sola Scriptura*—Scripture alone.

This position is declared clearly in the Lutheran confessions, documents adopted by Lutherans of the 16th century to proclaim boldly their Christian faith and their understanding of Holy Scripture. Some or all of these 11 confessions—published together in 1580 as the *Book of Concord*—still are subscribed today by Lutheran pastors and church bodies worldwide.

They define what it means to be Lutheran.

One of the confessions, the Formula of Concord, begins with these words: "We believe, teach, and confess that the prophetic and apostolic writings of the Old and New Testaments are the only rule and norm according to which all doctrines and teachers alike must be appraised and judged, as it is written in Ps. 119:105, 'Thy word is a lamp to my feet and a light to my path.'"

As Lutherans, we seek to be faithful to Holy Scripture and to the Lutheran confessions as a correct exposition of God's Word.

In this book, we will explore the principle teachings of Biblical Christianity under a common theme, "We Believe, Teach and Confess . . . ."

We begin with what God tells us in Scripture about His nature, how we can know Him and his creation of all that is—you and me included.

As we continue, our road map will be the first 21 articles of the Augsburg Confession. This is the chief confession of the Lutheran Church—written in 1530 and read to Emperor Charles V of the Holy Roman Empire as a statement of what Lutherans believe. Its first 21 articles deal with teachings of historic Christianity. The full text in translation is printed at the beginning of this book.

"Why are we here? What is the purpose of our existence? The answers change in each generation, but the questions are eternal." So concluded Newsweek's cover story.

Where humans *look* for answers may indeed change from one generation to the next, but the true answers—God's answers—to those and other spiritual questions do not change. "The word of our God stands forever," writes the prophet Isaiah (Is. 40:8). The apostle Peter repeats Isaiah's confession (1 Pet. 2:25). Peter adds: "And this is the word that was preached to you."

THE AUGSBURG CONFESSION

A Confession of Faith Presented in Augsburg by certain Princes and Cities to His Imperial Majesty Charles V in the Year 1530

Ps. 119:46

"I will also speak of thy testimonies before kings, and shall not be put to shame."

Preface

Most serene, most mighty, invincible Emperor, most gracious Lord:

A short time ago Your Imperial Majesty graciously summoned a diet of the empire to convene here in Augsburg. In the summons Your Majesty indicated an earnest desire to deliberate concerning matters pertaining to the Turk, that traditional foe of ours and of the Christian religion, and how with continuing help he might effectively be resisted. The desire was also expressed for deliberation on what might be done about the dissension concerning our holy faith and the Christian religion, and to this end it was proposed to employ all diligence amicably and charitably to hear, understand, and weigh the judgments, opinions, and beliefs of the several parties among us to unite the same in agreement on one Christian truth, to put aside whatever may not have been rightly interpreted or treated by either side, to have all of us embrace and adhere to a single, true religion and live together in unity and in one fellowship and church, even as we are all enlisted under one Christ. Inasmuch as we, the undersigned elector and princes and our associates, have been summoned for these purposes, together with other electors, princes, and estates, we have complied with the command and can say without boasting that we were among the first to arrive.

In connection with the matter pertaining to the faith and in conformity with the imperial summons, Your Imperial Majesty also graciously and earnestly requested that each of the electors, princes, and estates should commit to writing and present, in German and Latin, his judgments, opinions, and beliefs with reference to the said errors, dissensions, and abuses. Accordingly, after due deliberation and counsel, it was decided last Wednesday that, in keeping with Your Majesty's wish, we should present our case in German and Latin today (Friday). Wherefore, in dutiful obedience to Your Imperial Majesty, we offer and present a confession of our pastors' and preachers' teaching and of our own faith, setting forth how and in what manner, on the basis of the Holy Scriptures, these things are preached, taught, communicated, and embraced in our lands, principalities, dominions, cities and territories.

If the other electors, princes, and estates also submit a similar written statement of their judgments and opinions, in Latin and German, we are prepared, in obedience to Your Imperial Majesty, our most gracious lord, to discuss with them and their associates, in so far as this can honorably be done, such practical and equitable ways as may restore unity. Thus the matters at issue between us may be presented in writing on both sides, they may be discussed amicably and charitably, our differences may be reconciled, and we may be united in one, true religion, even as we are all under one Christ and should confess and contend for Christ. All of this is in accord with Your Imperial Majesty's aforementioned summons. That it may be done according to divine truth we invoke almighty God in deepest humility and implore him to bestow his grace to this end. Amen.

If, however, our lords, friends, and associates who represent the electors, princes, and estates of the other party do not comply with the procedure intended by Your Imperial Majesty's summons, if no amicable and charitable negotiations take place between us, and if no results are attained, nevertheless we on our part shall not omit doing anything, in so far as God and conscience allow, that may serve the cause of Christian unity. Of this Your Imperial Majesty, our aforementioned friends (the electors, princes, and estates), and every lover of the Christian religion who is concerned about these questions will be graciously and sufficiently assured from what follows in the confession which we and our associates submit.

In the past Your Imperial Majesty graciously gave assurance to the electors, princes, and estates of the empire, especially in a public instruction at the diet in Spires in 1526, that for reasons there stated Your Imperial Majesty was not disposed to render decisions in matters pertaining to our holy faith but would diligently urge it upon the pope to call a council. Again, by means of a written instruction at the last diet in Spires a year ago, the electors, princes, and estates of the empire were, among other things, informed and notified by Your Imperial Majesty's viceroy (His Royal Majesty of Hungary and Bohemia, etc.) and by Your Imperial Majesty's orator and appointed commissioners, that Your Imperial Majesty's viceroy, administrators, and councilors of the imperial government (together with the absent electors, princes, and representatives of the estates) who were assembled at the diet convened in Ratisbon had considered the proposal concerning a general council and acknowledged that it would be profitable to have such a council called. Since the relations between Your Imperial Majesty and the pope were improving and were progressing toward a good, Christian understanding, Your Imperial Majesty was sure that the pope would not refuse to call a general council, and so Your Imperial Majesty graciously offered to promote and bring about the calling of such a general council by the pope, along with Your Imperial Majesty, at the earliest opportunity and to allow no hindrance to be put in the way.

If the outcome should be such as we mentioned above, we offer in full obedience, even beyond what is required, to participate in such a general, free, and Christian council as the electors, princes, and estates have with the highest and best motives requested in all the diets of the empire which have been held during Your Imperial Majesty's reign. We have at various times made our protestations and appeals concerning these most weighty matters, and have done so in legal form and procedure. To these we declare our continuing adherence, and we shall not be turned aside from our position by these or any following negotiations (unless the matters in dissension are finally heard, amicably weighed, charitably settled, and brought to Christian concord in accordance with Your Imperial Majesty's summons) as we herewith publicly witness and assert. This is our confession and that of our associates, and it is specifically stated, article by article, in what follows.

Articles of Faith and Doctrine (German)

1. [God]
1 We unanimously hold and teach, in accordance with the decree of the Council of Nicaea, 2 that there is one divine essence, which is called and which is truly God, and that there are three persons in this one divine essence, equal in power and alike eternal: God the Father, God the Son, God the Holy Spirit. 3 All three are one divine essence, eternal, without division, without end, of infinite power, wisdom, and goodness, one creator and preserver of all things visible and invisible. 4 The word "person" is to be understood as the Fathers employed the term in this connection, not as a part or a property of another but as that which exists of itself.

5 Therefore all the heresies which are contrary to this article are rejected. Among these are the heresy of the Manichaeans, who assert that there are two gods, one good and one evil; also that of the Valentinians, Arians, Eunomians, Mohammedans, and others like them; 6 also that of the Samosatenes, old and new, who hold that there is only one person and sophistically assert that the other two, the Word and the Holy Spirit, are not necessarily distinct persons but that the Word signifies a physical word or voice and that the Holy Spirit is a movement induced in creatures.

2. [Original Sin]
1 It is also taught among us that since the fall of Adam all men who are born according to the course of nature are conceived and born in sin. That is, all men are full of evil lust and inclinations from their mothers' wombs and are unable by nature to have true fear of God and true faith in God. 2 Moreover, this inborn sickness and hereditary sin is truly sin and condemns to the eternal wrath of God all those who are not born again through Baptism and the Holy Spirit.

3 Rejected in this connection are the Pelagians and others who deny that original sin is sin, for they hold that natural man is made righteous by his own powers, thus disparaging the sufferings and merit of Christ.

3. [The Son of God]

1 It is also taught among us that God the Son became man, born of the virgin Mary, 2 and that the two natures, divine and human, are so inseparably united in one person that there is one Christ, true God and true man, who was truly born, suffered, was crucified, died, 3 and was buried in order to be a sacrifice not only for original sin but also for all other sins and to propitiate God's wrath. 4 The same Christ also descended into hell, truly rose from the dead on the third day, ascended into heaven, and sits on the right hand of God, that he may eternally rule and have dominion over all creatures, that through the Holy Spirit he may sanctify, purify, strengthen, and comfort all who believe in him, 5 that he may bestow on them life and every grace and blessing, and that he may protect and defend them against the devil and against sin. 6 The same Lord Christ will return openly to judge the living and the dead, as stated in the Apostles' Creed.

4. [Justification]

1 It is also taught among us that we cannot obtain forgiveness of sin and righteousness before God by our own merits, works, or satisfactions, but that we receive forgiveness of sin and become righteous before God by grace, for Christ's sake, through faith, 2 when we believe that Christ suffered for us and that for his sake our sin is forgiven and righteousness and eternal life are given to us. 3 For God will regard and reckon this faith as righteousness, as Paul says in Romans 3:21-26 and 4:5.

5. [The Office of the Ministry]

1 To obtain such faith God instituted the office of the ministry, that is, provided the Gospel and the sacraments. 2 Through these, as through means, he gives the Holy Spirit, who works faith, when and where he pleases, in those who hear the Gospel. 3 And the Gospel teaches that we have a gracious God, not by our own merits but by the merit of Christ, when we believe this.

4 Condemned are the Anabaptists and others who teach that the Holy Spirit comes to us through our own preparations, thoughts, and works without the external word of the Gospel.

6. [The New Obedience]

1 It is also taught among us that such faith should produce good fruits and good works and that we must do all such good works as God has commanded, but we should do them for God's sake and not place our trust in them as if thereby to merit favor before God. 2 For we receive forgiveness of sin and righteousness through faith in Christ, as Christ himself says, "So you also, when you have done all that is commanded you, say, 'We are unworthy servants'" (Luke 17:10). 3 The Fathers also teach thus, for Ambrose says, "It is ordained of God that whoever

believes in Christ shall be saved, and he shall have forgiveness of sins, not through works but through faith alone, without merit."

7. [The Church]

1 It is also taught among us that one holy Christian church will be and remain forever. This is the assembly of all believers among who the Gospel is preached in its purity and the holy sacraments are administered according to the Gospel. 2 For it is sufficient for the true unity of the Christian church that the Gospel be preached in conformity with a pure understanding of it and that the sacraments be administered in accordance with the divine Word. 3 It is not necessary for the true unity of the Christian church that ceremonies, instituted by men, should be observed uniformly in all places. 4 It is as Paul says in Eph. 4:4, 5, "There is one body and one Spirit, just as you were called to the one hope that belongs to your call, one Lord, one faith, one baptism."

8. [What the Church Is]

1 Again, although the Christian church, properly speaking, is nothing else than the assembly of all believers and saints, yet because in this life many false Christians, hypocrites, and even open sinners remain among the godly, the sacraments are efficacious even if the priests who administer them are wicked men, for as Christ himself indicated, "The Pharisees sit on Moses' seat" (Matt. 23:2).

3 Accordingly the Donatists and all others who hold contrary views are condemned.

9. Baptism

1 It is taught among us that Baptism is necessary and that grace is offered through it. 2 Children, too, should be baptized, for in Baptism they are committed to God and become acceptable to him.

3 On this account the Anabaptists who teach that infant Baptism is not right are rejected.

10. The Holy Supper of Our Lord

1 It is taught among us that the true body and blood of Christ are really present in the Supper of our Lord under the form of bread and wine and are there distributed and received. 2 The contrary doctrine is therefore rejected.

11. Confession

1 It is taught among us that private absolution should be retained and not allowed to fall into disuse. However, in confession it is not necessary to enumerate all trespasses and sins, 2 for this is impossible. Ps. 19:12, "Who can discern his errors?"

12. Repentance

1 It is taught among us that those who sin after Baptism receive forgiveness of sin whenever they come to repentance, 2 and absolution should not be denied them by the church. 3 Properly speaking, true repentance is nothing else than to have contrition and sorrow, or terror, on account of 5 sin, and yet at the same time to believe the Gospel and absolution (namely, that sin has been forgiven and grace has been obtained through Christ), and this faith will comfort the heart and again set it at rest. 6 Amendment of life and the forsaking of sin would then follow, for these must be the fruits of repentance, as John says, "Bear fruit that befits repentance" (Matt. 3:8).

7 Rejected here are those who teach that persons who have once become godly cannot fall again.

9 Condemned on the other hand are the Novatians who denied absolution to such as had sinned after Baptism.

10 Rejected also are those who teach that forgiveness of sin is not obtained through faith but through the satisfactions made by man.

13. The Use of the Sacraments

1 It is taught among us that the sacraments were instituted not only to be signs by which people might be identified outwardly as Christians, but that they are signs and testimonies of God's will toward us for the purpose of awakening and strengthening our faith. 2 For this reason they require faith, and they are rightly used when they are received in faith and for the purpose of strengthening faith.

14. Order in the Church

It is taught among us that nobody should publicly teach or preach or administer the sacraments in the church without a regular call.

15. Church Usages

1 With regard to church usages that have been established by men, it is taught among us that those usages are to be observed which may be observed without sin and which contribute to peace and good order in the church, among them being certain holy days, festivals, and the like. 2 Yet we accompany these observances with instruction so that consciences may not be burdened by the notion that such things are necessary for salvation. 3 Moreover it is taught that all ordinances and traditions instituted by men for the purpose of propitiating God and earning grace are contrary to the Gospel and the teaching about faith in Christ. 4 Accordingly monastic vows and other traditions concerning distinction of foods, days, etc., by which it is intended to earn grace and make satisfaction for sin, are useless and contrary to the Gospel.

16. Civil Government

1 It is taught among us that all government in the world and all estab-

lished rule and laws were instituted and ordained by God for the sake of good order, 2 and that Christians may without sin occupy civil offices or serve as princes and judges, render decisions and pass sentence according to imperial and other existing laws, punish evildoers with the sword, engage in just wars, serve as soldiers, buy and sell, take required oaths, possess property, be married, etc.

3 Condemned here are the Anabaptists who teach that none of the things indicated above is Christian.

4 Also condemned are those who teach that Christian perfection requires the forsaking of house and home, wife and child, and the renunciation of such activities as are mentioned above. Actually, true perfection consists alone of proper fear of God and real faith in God, for the Gospel does not teach an outward and temporal but an inward and eternal mode of existence and righteousness of the heart. 5 The Gospel does not overthrow civil authority, the state, and marriage but requires that all these be kept as true orders of God and that everyone, each according to his own calling, manifest Christian love and genuine good works in his station of life. 6 Accordingly Christians are obliged to be subject to civil authority and obey its commands and laws in all that can be done without sin. 7 But when commands of the civil authority cannot be obeyed without sin, we must obey God rather than men (Acts 5:29).

17. [The Return of Christ to Judgment]

1 It is also taught among us that our Lord Jesus Christ will return on the last day for judgment and will raise up all the dead, 2 to give eternal life and everlasting joy to believers and the elect 3 but to condemn ungodly men and the devil to hell and eternal punishment.

4 Rejected, therefore, are the Anabaptists who teach that the devil and condemned men will not suffer eternal pain and torment.

5 Rejected, too, are certain Jewish opinions which are even now making an appearance and which teach that, before the resurrection of the dead, saints and godly men will possess a worldly kingdom and annihilate all the godless.

18. Freedom of the Will

1 It is also taught among us that man possesses some measure of freedom of the will which enables him to live an outwardly honorable life and to make choices among the things that reason comprehends. 2 But without the grace, help, and activity of the Holy Spirit man is not capable of making himself acceptable to God, of fearing God and believing in God with his whole heart, or of expelling inborn evil lusts from his heart. 3 This is accomplished by the Holy Spirit, who is given through the Word of God, for Paul says in 1 Cor. 2:14, "Natural man does not receive the gifts of the Spirit of God."

4 In order that it may be evident that this teaching is no novelty, the clear words of Augustine on free will are here quoted from the third book of his Hypognosticon: "We concede that all men have a free will, for all

have a natural, innate understanding and reason. However, this does not enable them to act in matters pertaining to God (such as loving God with their whole heart or fearing him), for it is only in the outward acts of this life that they have freedom to choose good or evil. 5 By good I mean what they are capable of by nature: whether or not to labor in the fields, whether or not to eat or drink or visit a friend, whether to dress or undress, whether to build a house, take a wife, engage in a trade, or do whatever else may be good and profitable. 6 None of these is or exists without God, but all things are from him and through him. 7 On the other hand, by his own choice man can also undertake evil, as when he wills to kneel before an idol, commit murder, etc."

19. The Cause of Sin

It is taught among us that although almighty God has created and still preserves nature, yet sin is caused in all wicked men and despisers of God by the perverted will. This is the will of the devil and of all ungodly men; as soon as God withdraws his support, the will turns away from God to evil. It is as Christ says in John 8:44, "When the devil lies, he speaks according to his own nature."

20. Faith and Good Works

1 Our teachers have been falsely accused of forbidding good works. 2 Their writings on the Ten Commandments, and other writings as well, show that they have given good and profitable accounts and instructions concerning true Christian estates and works. 3 About these little was taught in former times, when for the most part sermons were concerned with childish and useless works like rosaries, the cult of saints, monasticism, pilgrimages, appointed fasts, holy days, brotherhoods, etc. 4 Our opponents no longer praise these useless works so highly as they once did, 5 and they have also learned to speak now of faith, about which they did not preach at all in former times. 6 They do not teach now that we become righteous before God by our works alone, but they add faith in Christ and say that faith and works make us righteous before God. 7 This teaching may offer a little more comfort than the teaching that we are to rely solely on our works.

8 Since the teaching about faith, which is the chief article in the Christian life, has been neglected so long (as all must admit) while nothing but works was preached everywhere, our people have been instructed as follows:

9 We begin by teaching that our works cannot reconcile us with God or obtain grace for us, for this happens only through faith, that is, when we believe that our sins are forgiven for Christ's sake, who alone is the mediator who reconciles the Father. 10 Whoever imagines that he can accomplish this by works, or that he can merit grace, despises Christ and seeks his own way to God, contrary to the Gospel.

11 This teaching about faith is plainly and clearly treated by Paul in

many passages, especially in Eph. 2:8, 9, "For by grace you have been saved through faith; and this is not your own doing, it is the gift of God — not because of works, lest any man should boast," etc.

12 That no new interpretation is here introduced can be demonstrated from Augustine, 13 who discusses this question thoroughly and teaches the same thing, namely, that we obtain grace and are justified before God through faith in Christ and not through works. His whole book, *De spiritu et litera*, proves this.

15 Although this teaching is held in great contempt among untried people, yet it is a matter of experience that weak and terrified consciences find it most comforting and salutary. The conscience cannot come to rest and peace through works, but only through faith, that is, when it is assured and knows that for Christ's sake it has a gracious God, 16 as Paul says in Rom. 5:1, "Since we are justified by faith, we have peace with God."

19 In former times this comfort was not heard in preaching, but poor consciences were driven to rely on their own efforts, and all sorts of works were undertaken. 20 Some were driven by their conscience into monasteries in the hope that there they might merit grace through monastic life. 21 Others devised other works for the purpose of earning grace and making satisfaction for sins. 22 Many of them discovered that they did not obtain peace by such means. It was therefore necessary to preach this doctrine about faith in Christ and diligently to apply it in order that men may know that the grace of God is appropriated without merits, through faith alone.

23 Instruction is also given among us to show that the faith here spoken of is not that possessed by the devil and the ungodly, who also believe the history of Christ's suffering and his resurrection from the dead, but we mean such true faith as believes that we receive grace and forgiveness of sin through Christ.

24 Whoever knows that in Christ he has a gracious God, truly knows God, calls upon him, and is not, like the heathen, without God. 25 For the devil and the ungodly do not believe this article concerning the forgiveness of sin, and so they are at enmity with God, cannot call upon him, and have no hope of receiving good from him. Therefore, as has just been indicated, the Scriptures speak of faith but do not mean by it such knowledge as the devil and ungodly men possess. Heb. 11:1 teaches about faith in such a way as to make it clear that faith is not merely a knowledge of historical events but is a confidence in God and in the fulfillment of his promises. 26 Augustine also reminds us that we would understand the word "faith" in the Scriptures to mean confidence in God, assurance that God is gracious to us, and not merely such a knowledge of historical events as the devil also possesses.

27 It is also taught among us that good works should and must be done, not that we are to rely on them to earn grace but that we may do God's will and glorify him. 28 It is always faith alone that apprehends

grace and forgiveness of sin. 29 When through faith the Holy Spirit is given, the heart is moved to do good works. 31 Before that, when it is without the Holy Spirit, the heart is too weak. 32 Moreover, it is in the power of the devil, who drives poor human beings into many sins. 33 We see this in the philosophers who undertook to lead honorable and blameless lives; they failed to accomplish this, and instead fell into many great and open sins. 34 This is what happens when a man is without true faith and the Holy Spirit and governs himself by his own human strength alone.

35 Consequently this teaching concerning faith is not to be accused of forbidding good works but is rather to be praised for teaching that good works are to be done and for offering help as to how they may be done. 36 For without faith and without Christ human nature and human strength are much too weak to do good works, 37 call upon God, have patience in suffering, love one's neighbor, diligently engage in callings which are commanded, render obedience, avoid evil lusts, etc. 38 Such great and genuine works cannot be done without the help of Christ, 39 as he himself says in John 15:5, "Apart from me you can do nothing."

21. The Cult of Saints

1 It is also taught among us that saints should be kept in remembrance so that our faith may be strengthened when we see what grace they received and how they were sustained by faith. Moreover, their good works are to be an example for us, each of us in his own calling. So His Imperial Majesty may in salutary and godly fashion imitate the example of David in making war on the Turk, for both are incumbents of a royal office which demands the defense and protection of their subjects.

2 However, it cannot be proved from the Scriptures that we are to invoke saints or seek help from them. "For there is one mediator between God and men, Christ Jesus" (1 Tim. 2:5), who is the only saviour, the only highpriest, advocate, and intercessor before God (Rom. 8:34). He alone has promised to hear our prayers. 3 Moreover, according to the Scriptures, the highest form of divine service is sincerely to seek and call upon this same Jesus Christ in every time of need. 4 "If anyone sins, we have an advocate with the Father, Jesus Christ the righteous" (1 John 2:1).

1 This is just about a summary of the doctrines that are preached and taught in our churches for proper Christian instruction, the consolation of consciences, and the amendment of believers. Certainly we would not wish to put our own souls and consciences in grave peril before God by misusing his name or Word, nor should we wish to bequeath to our children and posterity any other teaching than that which agrees with the pure Word of God and Christian truth. Since this teaching is grounded clearly on the Holy Scriptures and is not contrary or opposed to that of the universal Christian church, or even of the Roman church (in so far

as the latter's teaching is reflected in the writings of the Fathers), we think that our opponents cannot disagree with us in the articles set forth above. Therefore, those who presume to reject, avoid, and separate from our churches as if our teaching were heretical, act in an unkind and hasty fashion, contrary to all Christian unity and love, and do so without any solid basis of divine command or Scripture. 2 The dispute and dissension are concerned chiefly with various traditions and abuses. Since, then, there is nothing unfounded or defective in the principal articles and since this our confession is seen to be godly and Christian, the bishops should in all fairness act more leniently, even if there were some defect among us in regard to traditions, although we hope to offer firm grounds and reasons why we have changed certain traditions and abuses.

THE ONE TRUE GOD AND HIS CREATION (ARTICLE 1)

David L. Mahsman

To find spiritual meaning, one must know God. Fortunately, He has told us about Himself and why we are here.

According to researcher George Barna, only seven of every 10 adult Americans today "adopt the traditional view of God."

That's not to say that even all those with the "traditional" view necessarily hold the Biblical view of God. The statement tested by Barna was, "God is the all-powerful, all-knowing, perfect creator of the universe who rules the world today."

Honest seekers can come pretty close to agreeing with such a statement simply by looking around and drawing their own conclusions.

Nature, for example, tells us something about God.

The order in the universe—the regularity of day and night, the rhythm of the seasons, the balance of nature—and the intricate workings of the human mind and body offer strong proof that an intelligent and powerful mind is behind it all. There is even something "spiritual" about the awe we feel at the first sight of the Grand Canyon's magnificence, the power of Niagara Falls, or the glorious beauty of fall color in New England.

The apostle Paul says as much when he writes that "since the creation of the world God's invisible qualities—his eternal power and divine nature—have been clearly seen, being understood from what has been made . . ." (Rom. 1:20).

We even carry within ourselves evidence of the divine. The human conscience, that innate knowledge of right and wrong, tells us that there is a God and that we are accountable to Him (Rom. 2:15).

God Tells Us about Himself

That there is a God who created and still sustains all things, and who is wise and powerful and good, is evident. But knowing a few things about the nature of God isn't enough.

The fact is that we can know—actually *know*—precious little about the true God unless He reveals Himself to us. But here's some good news: God *has* revealed Himself to us.

This revelation is found in Holy Scripture and in the person of Jesus Christ. "In the past God spoke to our forefathers through the prophets at many times and in various ways, but in these last days he has spoken to us by his Son, whom he appointed heir of all things, and through whom he made the universe" (Heb. 1:1,2).

First of all, God tells us that He isn't a *what*, but a *who*. He tells us that He *is*. He calls Himself "I am" (Ex. 3:14), a name, by the way, that Jesus used in claiming Himself to be God: "'I tell you the truth,' Jesus answered, 'before Abraham was born, I am!'"(John 8:58).

God tells us about His essential nature, that He is one God (Deut. 6:4; 1 Cor. 8:4), one indivisible essence, but in three distinct persons: Father, Son and Holy Spirit (Matt. 28:19; 2 Cor. 13:14). The Father is fully God (1 Cor. 8:6); the Son, who became a man in the person of Jesus, is fully God (1 John 5:20; Rom. 9:5); and the Holy Spirit is fully God (Acts 5:3,4).

Still, there are not three Gods, but one God. As Article 1 of the Augsburg Confession puts it, "All three are one divine essence, eternal, without division, without end, of infinite power, wisdom, and goodness, one creator and preserver of all things visible and invisible."

Now, we could never have figured *that* out by ourselves. In fact, our minds aren't able to really comprehend the three-in-one nature of God even as God reveals it to us!

But this *is* how God reveals Himself to us, which makes any other concept of God a product of human imagination and nothing less than idolatrous. Thus, we must reject any other notion of God, whether it sounds vaguely Christian (such as those offered by the Unitarians, Mormons or Jehovah's Witnesses) or not (as in other world religions or in the New Age Movement, for example).

God also tells us that He is eternal (Ps. 90:1,2); unchanging (Mal. 3:6); all-powerful (Luke 1:37); all-knowing (John 21:17); present everywhere (Jer. 23:24); holy and sinless (Lev. 19:2); entirely just, fair and impartial (Deut. 32:4); always faithful to His promises (2 Tim. 2:13); entirely good and kind (Ps. 145:9); merciful (Ps. 145:9); and gracious, loving and forgiving (Ex. 34:6,7; 1 John 4:8).

God's Creative Work

Let's look at what God has to say about how He made the world, the universe, everything—including you and me.

Using Moses as His human agent, God provides a completely reliable account of His creative activity. The only One who was actually present at the creation offers an overview of His own work in Gen. 1:1 to 2:3. Then, beginning with Gen. 2:4, He gives a more detailed account of the creation of man and woman, Adam and Eve, our first parents.

We learn there that we are not the product of chance evolution. We are not the descendants of some lower forms of life. That certainty is founded firmly on the truthfulness of God and His Word (although evolutionary models have problems even apart from contradicting the Creator's account). There is purpose to our existence, because we were deliberately created by a wise and loving God.

Our common ancestors—*everyone's* common ancestors—were real people, historical figures, specially created by God in a way different from the way He had created everything else that exists. God created Adam "from the dust of the ground and breathed into his nostrils the breath of life, and the man became a living being" (Gen. 2:7). Taking a rib from Adam, God created Eve. He brought her to Adam, who immediately recognized her as "bone of my bones and flesh of my flesh" (Gen. 2:23).

All else had been created by God out of nothing. He simply had said the word—"Let there be"—and it was: The raw materials—heaven, earth, water, light—on the first day; division of the waters above and below on the second; separation of land and sea and the creation of plant life on the third; the bearers of light and markers of time—the sun, moon and stars—on the fourth; fish, marine life and birds on the fifth; and animals on the sixth.

Although God could have brought everything into existence in a blink of an eye or stretched it out over time (something He also created), Genesis is clear that God chose to do His work in the course of six days. Still, Scripture (in Genesis and elsewhere) gives less attention to the creation of matter than to how God ordered creation to be a fit habitation for humankind.

It was on the sixth day that God created the first human beings.

"Let us make man in our image, in our likeness, and let them rule over the fish of the sea and the birds of the air, over the livestock, over all the earth, and over all the creatures that move along the ground," God counseled with Himself (Gen. 1:26). Moses continues, "So God created man in his own image, in the image of God he created him; male and female he created them."

Beyond the way in which they were made, Adam and Eve were unlike anything else in God's creation because they were created in the image of God—that is, in a state of righteousness, innocence, and blessedness.

God created humankind for Himself. The relationship among Adam, Eve and their Creator was one of perfect and intimate fellowship. The will and desire of our first parents were perfectly in accord with that of the One who had brought them into existence.

A Relationship Destroyed—And Restored

That relationship was destroyed when Adam and Eve listened to a fallen angel, Satan, and disobeyed the one command their Creator had given them—not to eat from the tree of the knowledge of good and evil. No longer did they bear the image of God.

Their act of disobedience has had its effect even on us, so that "since the fall of Adam all men who are propagated according to nature are born in sin" (AC 2). We remain accountable to our Creator for our every thought, word and action, but we no longer live as God demands.

The sin of our first parents totally corrupted God's good creation. It is at the root of all the death and misery in this world. *All* of creation, which was designed to respond to its Creator, has been "groaning" ever since sin entered it (Rom. 8:22).

But the Creator did not abandon His creation.

First of all, God has made provision for the continuation of His creation, which, in spite of our sin, He also preserves.

We are told in Genesis that God created all living things—plant, animal and human—to propagate themselves. Of Adam and Eve, for example, it is written that "God blessed them and said to them, 'Be fruitful and increase in number; fill the earth and subdue it . . .'" (Gen. 1:28).

Still, it is God who continues to create. And to know that we are creatures of God gives us worth. It lifts us up to confess with Martin Luther, "I believe that God has made me and all creatures; that He has given me my body and soul, eyes, ears, and all my members, my reason and all my senses, and still takes care of them."

God continues to look after His creation. Not only did He so order creation to provide all that His creatures need, but creation continues to exist strictly through the power of God's Word (see Heb. 1:3).

"All this He does only out of fatherly, divine goodness and mercy, without any merit or worthiness in me," Luther writes of God's creation and preservation in the *Small Catechism*. "For all this it is my duty to thank and praise, serve and obey Him."

More than all that, though, God has provided for the restoration of creation—including you and me—to its original purity and perfection. To do that, the Creator humbled Himself and became one of us. In Jesus Christ, God fulfilled His promise of a Savior, a promise made on the very day that Adam and Eve fell into sin (Gen. 3:15).

Paul summarizes: "He [Christ] is the image of the invisible God, the firstborn over all creation. For by him all things were created: things in heaven and on earth, visible and invisible, whether thrones or powers or rulers or authorities; all things were created by him and for him. He is before all things, and in him all things hold together. And he is the head of the body, the church; he is the beginning and the firstborn from among the dead, so that in everything he might have the supremacy. For God was pleased to have all his fullness dwell in him, and through him to reconcile to himself all things, whether things on earth or things in heaven, by making peace through his blood shed on the cross" (Col. 1:15–20).

One day, the present heaven and earth will pass away, and a new heaven and earth that no longer groans under the weight of sin will take its place (see 2 Peter 3:10,13; Rev. 21:1ff.). Meanwhile, those who are brought to faith in Jesus Christ are forgiven their sins and become new creatures (2 Cor. 5:17). God's image begins to be renewed in them (Col. 3:10).

In Christ, God has restored our fellowship with Him. Like Adam and Eve before the fall, we once again can commune with our Creator. He speaks to us through His Word, provides direction for our lives, and invites us to speak to Him in prayer, promising to listen and to answer. And we shall live with Him eternally, just as He always intended.

FOR REFLECTION

1. From your experience, what are some common "notions" about God in our world today? Where do many people get their ideas about God?

2. Read Isaiah 43:1–3. What does God reveal about who He is and what He has done for His people?

3. Why is it critical that Christians confess God as "creator and preserver of all things visible and invisible"? What evidence of God's creative love comes to your mind when you think about God the creator?

4. In his explanation to the First Article of the Apostles' Creed, Luther writes, "I believe that God has made *me* . . . given *me* my body and soul . . . richly and daily provides *me* . . . defends *me*. . . ." In what ways is God's grace and goodness in Christ a blessing to you *personally* today?

5. Christians confess the triune God—one God in three persons. How is God, Father, Son and Holy Spirit, active in your daily life? In what ways does faith in the Trinity bring comfort and hope in the midst of life's problems?

FOR FURTHER READING

- Genesis 1:1–3:24
- The Athanasian Creed (*Lutheran Worship,* page 134)
- Luther's *Small Catechism,* First Article and Explanation

SIN (ARTICLES 2 AND 19)

Joel Lehenbauer

"Sin" isn't so much the bad things that we do. Rather, it's at the very root of what we are.

Culture-watchers everywhere seem to agree: after decades of a declining interest in things spiritual, as *Newsweek* once put it, "now it's suddenly OK, even chic, to use the S-words—soul, sacred, spiritual, sin." That last S-word, sin, may be most surprising of all.

Today's seekers may be more willing to use the word "sin." But they seem less able than ever to say for sure what it is or what it means for their lives.

According to a survey by the Barna Group, even most "evangelical" young people today admit that they are "confused" about how to tell right from wrong. Fifty-seven percent of church-affiliated youth said that no objective standard of truth exists, and only 15 percent disagreed with the statement, "What is right for one person in a given situation might not be right for another person who encounters the same situation."

This new openness to talk about sin, along with the uncertainty about how to define it, presents the church with a tremendous opportunity.

Some, no doubt, will ask whether it makes sense to pursue this subject at all in view of our "tune it out, turn it off" society. Despite the return of the "S-words," most people today still find serious discussion of sin uncomfortable, offensive or simply irrelevant. Wouldn't it be better to focus on the "positive" aspects of the Biblical message—God's love, forgiveness and acceptance?

Certainly, sharing the message of God's love in Christ must always be the church's primary concern. That's why it's so important to help people understand what the Bible says about sin, since people who don't take sin seriously will never understand their serious need for a Savior or the seriousness of God's love in Christ.

We may choose to use, like Scripture itself, any number of expressions or illustrations to explain what "sin" is. But we can't omit the message. As Jesus said, "It is not the healthy who need a doctor, but the sick. . . . I have come not to call the righteous, but sinners" (Matt. 9:12). Martin Luther is right: "If you want to engage profitably in the study of theology and Holy Scripture and do not want to run head-on into a Scripture closed and sealed, then learn, above all things, to understand sin rightly."

Wrong Ideas about Sin

Like looking in a mirror, facing up to sin means taking an honest look at *ourselves*. And wrong understandings of sin almost always involve a foggy picture of "who we are" as human beings.

It's possible, on the one hand, to fall prey to a morbid pessimism about life and humanity that, if left unchecked, can result in sheer cynicism and despair. Consider the advice given by one modern-day "spiritual mentor": "We should repeat to ourselves, every day, I am one of the billions dragging himself across earth's surface. One, and no more. This banality justifies any conclusion, any behavior or action: debauchery, chastity, suicide, work, crime, sloth or rebellion. Whence it follows that each man is right to do what he does."

Scripture is diametrically opposed to this destructive, distorted view of self and human behavior. According to the Bible, life is *not* meaningless. Individuals are *not* worthless specks in a disinterested universe. A person's actions and decisions *are* important—to God, to others and to one's self.

On the opposite extreme is the naive, overly optimistic view of life and self found in many of today's most popular "self-help" guidebooks. As one best-selling author gushes, "I practice awe. I mean I'm in awe of the dishes, I'm in awe of my liver, I'm in awe when I play tennis, I'm in awe of it all. I'm just awestruck with the magnificence and the miraculousness and the bliss that is in this world."

There is, of course, something right—even Biblical—about this sense of "awe" at God's creation (see Ps. 139:13–14). Being in awe of your dishes, however, won't keep them from breaking. Being in awe of your liver won't protect it from cancer. Being in awe of all of the "bliss" and beauty in the world won't eliminate (or even explain) all of the ugly and awful realities of life—war, violence, poverty, abuse.

And being in "awe" of one's self won't take away the angry thoughts, bitter memories, hurtful feelings and foolish actions that so often make our own lives far from "blissful."

We need more than just any "best seller" to show us the truth about ourselves and our sin. We need the best-seller of all time—the Bible.

The Truth about Sin

The Bible tells it like it is—the good, the bad, the ugly and God's answer to all that is wrong with us and the world. It tells how God created the world without a single flaw or imperfection, and how God's most precious creation, Adam and Eve, originally lived in perfect harmony with Him and all He had made.

It tells how the Evil One, not content to serve as one of God's "ministering spirits," rebelled against his Creator and seduced our first parents with his lies. The Ancient Serpent convinced Adam and Eve that the true path to "godhood" meant disobeying God and declaring their "independence" from Him. This first sin, like all those to follow, was at its core a sin of unbelief: a willful turning from trust in God to trust in self. The results of this faithless act were immediate and devastating, and can be summed up in one word: death.

Though Adam and Eve did not drop dead the moment they sinned, the seeds of physical death were now planted in the whole human race. Far worse, they died spiritually—they cut themselves off from their only Source of life, joy and peace. Try as they might, they could no longer trust the One who had created them in His own image. Instead of loving Him, they now hated Him. Instead of running to Him, they fled from Him. Instead of confiding in Him, they lied to Him. Their truest Friend now looked for all the world like their greatest enemy, and they were helpless to do anything about it.

The story is told of a man attending church for the first time who turned to his friend and whispered, "What's this business of 'sin' the pastor keeps talking about?" His friend replied, "I think it has something to do with Adam and Eve." "Oh," said the first, noticeably relieved, "then it doesn't have anything to do with us."

Wrong, says the Bible—dead wrong. No event in history has ever had more to do with us than the sin of our first parents. To paraphrase a sainted theologian: Everything follows the seeds of its own nature. No cawing crow ever produced a cooing dove nor ferocious lion a gentle lamb, and no man polluted with inborn sin ever begets a holy child.

The Root Issue

In the words of one of our Lutheran Confessions, the Smalcald Articles, we, too, "must confess what Saint Paul says in Rom. 5,12, namely, that sin had its origin in one man, Adam, through whose disobedience all men were made sinners and became subject to death and the devil. This is called original sin, or root sin."

Note the word "root." When we hear the word "sin," we probably think of one or more wrong acts—we focus on the "fruits" instead of the "roots," the symptoms rather than the real problem. Recalling the words of Jesus in Matt. 12:33, Luther points out that "we are not sinners because we commit sin—now this one, now that one—but we commit these acts because we are sinners before we do so . . . a bad tree and bad seed produce bad fruit, and from an evil root nothing but an evil tree can grow."

Just how bad is our sinful condition? Far worse, according to Luther, than we can ever know or imagine. "By special benefit of divine goodness," he says, "no one fully and perfectly understands and feels what sin and the power of the Law really are. If conscience truly touched and tormented a man, if he truly felt the gravity and the enormity of sin, he would not live long if indeed he did not suddenly die."

What we *can* know is bad enough. Because of original sin, says the Augsburg Confession, we are "unable by nature to have true fear of God and true faith in God." Not only are we powerless to trust God, we are also "full of evil lust from our mothers' wombs"—"programmed" from conception to rebel against Him.

Our heart, mind, and will are so perverted by sin that we prefer the hateful taunts of Satan, the world and our own sinful flesh to the kind and loving voice of God. As a result, like water belching from a poisoned spring, "out of the heart come evil thoughts, murder, adultery, sexual immorality, theft, false testimony, slander" (Matt. 15:19) and all sorts of "actual sins"—corrupt thoughts, words and deeds—that God's Law clearly reveals as contrary to His holy will.

But the worst news by far is that "this inborn sickness and hereditary sin . . . condemns to the eternal wrath of God" (AC 2). While this truth, too (especially!), must be spoken in love (Eph. 4:15), there is nothing "loving" about glossing over it or avoiding it. Sin kills. Sin damns. Sin condemns a person to everlasting hell—final and total separation from God. That's why we need to take sin so seriously—and deal seriously with it.

God's Solution

But how? What can we do about sin? Scripture's shocking answer is—nothing. (What, after all, can a dead person do?) "Feeling bad" about sin won't change a person's sinful nature. Blaming others, making excuses or "thinking positively" only make it harder to face the truth. And the most tireless and sincere striving and resolving to "do better" can't accomplish a thing, since "no one"—*no one*—"will be declared righteous in God's sight by observing the law" (Rom. 3:20).

All we can "do," in fact, is admit that there is nothing we can do. That's what the Bible means by "repentance": humbly and honestly admitting that what God says about us is true, and that there is nothing—nothing at all—that we can do to help or save ourselves. The only proper response to Scripture's message about sin is that of the tax collector in Jesus' parable: "God, have mercy on me, a sinner" (Luke 18:13).

Only from this prostrate position can we see what God so fervently wants to show us: not only *can* we do nothing about our sin, we *need* do nothing. Why? Because God has done it all for us through His Son, Jesus Christ. God shows us our sickness to show us our Healer. He shows us our lostness and helplessness to show us our Savior and Helper. He "kills" us with the message of sin to make us alive through the message of His Son, the Lamb of God who takes away the sin of the world (John 1:30).

Listen to Luther: "The Law lays my sins on me, but God takes them from me and lays them on the Lamb. There they lie well, better than on me. And God means to say: 'I see that sin weighs heavily on you and that you would have to break down under the heavy burden; but I will relieve you of it, take the sin from your back . . . and out of pure grace lay it on the shoulders of this Lamb.' . . . Let this picture be precious to you. It makes Christ a servant of sins, yea, a Bearer of sins, the lowliest, the most despised of men, who Himself destroys all sin and says: 'I am come to serve others, not to let Myself be served."

Strange as it may sound, a discussion of sin must stress, above all, that sin is *not* the central message of Scripture. The Bible's central message is the forgiveness of sin won for the whole world by the life, death and resurrection of Jesus Christ.

So much more could be said about this forgiveness and the "new life" that it gives. We are reborn as new creatures in Holy Baptism. Repenting daily and claiming God's forgiveness, we are enabled to serve Him and others in love. Through Word and Sacrament, God's Spirit empowers us to "fight the good fight" against the devil, the world and our flesh.

The Gospel, too, enables us to rejoice in the certainty that someday all striving and sighing over sin will cease, and we, white-robed, will join the heavenly choir in singing: "Worthy is the Lamb, who was slain, to receive power and wealth and wisdom and strength and honor and glory and praise! To him who sits on the throne and to the Lamb be praise and honor and glory and power, for ever and ever!" (Rev. 12:13). Amen!

FOR REFLECTION: SIN (ARTICLE 2)

1. What views of sin are common in our world today? In what ways do people deny or diminish the seriousness of human sinfulness?

2. Luther explains the First Commandment in the words, "We should fear, love, and trust God above all things." How is every sin a rebellion against the First Commandment ("You shall have no other gods")?

3. Read Romans 3:9–20. What are the similarities to the Ten Commandments? What is the purpose of God's law?

4. Why is it important that Christian preaching and teaching always include God's judgment against sinners? Why do Christians, too, need to hear the Law?

5. For believers in Christ, God's last word is not "guilty," but "not guilty." In what ways does Jesus' death and resurrection give you direction for living? strength for living?

FOR FURTHER READING

- Matthew 15:10–20
- Galatians 5:1–26
- *Luther's Small Catechism,* "Confession and Absolution"

Jesus Christ: 'His Only Son, Our Lord' (Article 3)

David A. Lumpp

Jesus Christ is fully God and fully man. That fact is essential to the
Christian faith and critical for our eternal well-being.

*"In Christ God was reconciling the world to himself, not counting
their trespasses against them" (2 Cor. 5:19, NRSV).*
The apostle Paul underscores the lengths to which God went to rescue
His fallen creatures from sin and death. At just the right time—at what
the Bible calls the "fullness of time" (Gal. 4:4)—He sent His only Son to
do for us what we could never hope to do for ourselves.

Because of what God has done in Jesus Christ, His Son, our sins are
forgiven. We are pronounced righteous in God's sight. We are redeemed.
We are reconciled to the Father, and we are restored to friendship with
Him.

This "Good News" is the heart of our faith and life, so clearly
expressed in the Augsburg Confession. Article 3 presents the Lutheran
understanding of the person of Christ as the very Son of God. It summarizes His work by highlighting the central events through which our
salvation is realized. As the article itself acknowledges, the rehearsal of
this "salvation history" borrows the familiar language of the Apostles'
Creed.

One Lord, One Faith

Thankfully, for all the theological disagreements of the 16th century,
there was no argument about the person of Jesus Christ. Such agreement
had been gradually attained in the early church only after considerable
debate about the meaning of the New Testament's affirmations and
descriptions of Jesus as a genuine man and also as the very Son of God
himself.

Once it was recognized on the basis of Scripture that the earthly Jesus
was in fact the eternal Son of God (John 1:1-3, 14-18) in whom "all the
fullness of the Deity lives in bodily form" (Col. 2:9), early Christians
turned their attention to the mystery of how one person could be both
fully God and fully human. They read the New Testament accounts of
Jesus doing and experiencing thoroughly human things—not to mention

those passages that actually affirm Jesus' true humanity (e.g., Heb. 2:14, 17–18). They also were familiar with the accounts of Jesus performing works that only God could do. Moreover, New Testament Christians called Jesus "Lord," or "*Kyrios,*" the Greek word for the saving, covenant God of the Old Testament. And the New Testament was abundantly clear about Jesus' equality with the Father and the Son (e.g., Matt. 28:19; John 10:29–30; 2 Cor. 13:14).

Most important, these efforts were not a matter of mere theological speculation or academic curiosity. The early church quickly realized that the Gospel itself was at stake in the answers it gave to these questions.

To forfeit either Jesus' true deity or His true humanity, or to permit one to be swallowed up by the other, would have distorted the New Testament witness and jeopardize the salvation Jesus came to bring. On the one hand, Jesus had to be a true man for Him truly to take the place of other human beings. As one fourth-century church father put it, "What was not assumed [true humanity] was not redeemed." On the other hand, Jesus had to be truly God if His sacrifice was to avail for all of humanity. Martin Luther reflected the consensus of the entire church when he declared that if Christ is robbed of His deity, then "there remains no help against God's wrath and no rescue from His judgment. Our sin, misery, and distress are so enormous. . . . For this *God's Son* had to become man, suffer, and shed His blood" (emphasis added).

Glory in the Cross

After a long struggle, the church came to confess in an explicit way that in the one person of Jesus there are two distinct—yet inseparable—natures. As the God-Man, He won for human beings forgiveness of sins, life and salvation. His victory came not in the typical way of conquest. Rather, Jesus reversed the usual measures of human achievement and attained victory through self-sacrifice.

St. Paul writes: "[Christ Jesus], being in very nature God, did not consider equality with God something to be grasped, but made himself nothing, taking the very nature of a servant, being made in human likeness. And being found in appearance as a man, he humbled himself and became obedient to death—even death on a cross!" (Phil. 2:6–8).

From His conception as a human being through His death and burial, the Son of God set aside full use of His divine majesty and power. This is often called His "state of humiliation." His "humiliation" ended and His "exaltation" began when Jesus returned to life in the grave. His resurrection is the Father's emphatic declaration that Jesus is the Son of God (Rom. 1:3–4) and that our sins are now in fact forgiven. "He was delivered over to death for our sins and was raised to life for our justification" (Rom. 4:25).

Such forgiveness is a present reality, not a future possibility. By the power of the Holy Spirit, Christians call the risen Jesus "Lord" (Acts 2:36)—and for good reason: "Therefore God exalted him to the highest place and gave him the name that is above every name, that at the name of Jesus every knew should bow, in heaven and on earth and under the earth, and every tongue confess that Jesus Christ is Lord, to the glory of God the Father" (Phil. 2:9–11).

The coming of the Son of God as a flesh-and-blood man (the "incarnation," John 1:14) was an act of sheer, undeserved mercy. It was not a response to or a reward for human preparation. God's reign through Jesus Christ is above all a rule of grace. Though the extent and power of His kingly rule are never in question, Jesus is *our* beneficent king because we have known His grace and love for *us*.

Indeed, shortly after Peter made his dramatic confession that Jesus was the Son of the living God (Matt. 16:16), Jesus began to explain that He would go to Jerusalem and "suffer many things," "be killed" and "on the third day be raised to life" (Matt. 16:21). This may have made little sense to disciples who expected a much different kind of king, but it is perfectly consistent for One who had not "come to be served, but to serve, and to give his life a ransom for many" (Mark 10:45).

No Condemnation

Since the fall, human beings are understandably disturbed by their sin and by the constricting grip it often has over their lives. Even Christian men and women know the reality of guilt and failure: "For what I do is not the good I want to do; no, the evil I do not want to do—this I keep on doing" (Rom. 7:19).

The serpent tempted Adam and Eve to doubt the words of God. That ultimate temptation is no less real today, when in the face of sin and guilt Christians conclude that the Gospel could not possibly be for them. The Gospel may be for everybody else, we sometimes reason, but somehow our guilt is too enormous and our doubt too persistent. "What a wretched man I am! Who will rescue me from this body of death?" (Rom. 7:24).

To troubled hearts like these, Martin Luther followed St. Paul's lead. He resorted not to more or better arguments. Instead, he stuck with the only Word that could possibly dislodge and overcome such fears and anxieties. The Word Luther repeated was the Gospel promise of God's forgiveness in Jesus Christ, the second Adam (Rom. 5:12–21). "Therefore, there is now no condemnation for those who are in Christ Jesus, because through Jesus Christ the law of the Spirit of life set me free from the law of sin and death" (Rom. 8:1–2).

Luther's favorite description for the Gospel was that of a "happy exchange": Jesus Christ has our sin with all of its debilitating effects dumped on His shoulders, while we are given His righteousness freely and unconditionally. "God made him who had no sin to be sin for us, so that in him we might become the righteousness of God." (2 Cor. 5:21)

How is God really disposed toward human beings? The *only* place to look for the answer is Jesus Christ. "For God so loved the world that he gave his one and only Son, that whoever believes in him shall not perish but have everlasting life. For God did not send his Son into the world to condemn the world, but to save the world through him" (John 3:16–17).

In the *Large Catechism,* Luther captured this reality in a poignant way. There, he called Jesus a "mirror of the Father's heart." To know how God regards His creatures—even His most wayward creatures—one need only look to the cross and empty tomb of His Son.

Yet even Christians have short and sometimes selective memories. God knows this. So He keeps reminding us that our salvation was no afterthought or "contingency plan." It was prepared for us in eternity (1 Peter 1:1–2).

In addition, we are much more than spectators in a battle waged by God against sin, death and the devil. Through the washing of Baptism, we, too, die to sin and rise with Jesus Christ (Rom. 6:3–4; Col. 2:12). Through the body and blood of God's Son that is ours in the Lord's Supper, we receive yet again the assurance that our sin is forgiven (Matt. 26:28), and we proclaim that God's victory has been decisively and irreversibly won (1 Cor. 11:26).

"To know Christ is to know His benefits," wrote Luther's associate, Philip Melanchthon. Those benefits are "known" through such otherwise ordinary means as words and water and bread and wine. But while the means are ordinary, the message they convey is anything but, for this message is a definitive promise of life with God himself.

The Bible's witness to Jesus as Son of God and Savior is of one piece. To understand this is to understand Christian doctrine in its beginning, its essence, and its end. Again, Luther got it exactly right: "All those who have correctly had and kept the chief article of Jesus Christ have remained safe and secure in the right Christian faith. . . . For whoever stands correctly and firmly in the belief that Jesus Christ is true God and man, that he died and has risen again for us, such a person has all other articles added to him and they firmly stand by him."

FOR REFLECTION

1. "Who do you say that I am?" Jesus asked his disciples (Matthew 16:13). What are some common views about Jesus today?

2. Jesus is both fully divine and fully human. Why is it necessary that the Savior of the world be true God? Why is it necessary that the Son of God be true man?

3. Read Philippians 2:5–11. What does Jesus' humiliation mean for Christians? What does His exaltation mean for your daily life?

4. Make a list of Jesus' titles (e.g., Lord, Redeemer, King, etc.). How does each title witness to His person and saving work? How does each title give you encouragement and strength for serving Him?

5. "To know Christ is to know His benefits?" What are His benefits for you today? How do we receive His benefits at worship? at home?

FOR FURTHER READING

- John 1:1–18
- Luther's *Small Catechism,* The Second Article
- Leslie Brandt, *Jesus/Now* (CPH)

JUSTIFICATION: WHAT IT'S ALL ABOUT (ARTICLE 4)

J. A. O. Preus III

God is our problem. He is also our Solution.

"What's it all about?"

Sooner or later, any honest seeker into Christianity will ask this question. This is perhaps the most important question any pastor or lay person gets asked by those inquiring into the faith: "What's it all about? What's at the heart of this faith called 'Christian'?"

Questions like these are on the minds of many people today, people who are seeking the inner meanings of life and existence, of God and humanity. "What's it all about?"

It's all about this: ". . . that we cannot obtain forgiveness of sin and righteousness before God by our own merits, works, or satisfactions, but that we receive forgiveness of sin and become righteous before God by grace, for Christ's sake, through faith, when we believe that Christ suffered for us and that for his sake our sin is forgiven and righteousness and eternal life are given to us. For God will regard and reckon this faith as righteousness, as Paul says in Romans 3:21–26 and 4:5" (AC 4).

Here is the heart of this faith called Christian. This is what it centers around, what it hangs upon. This is what makes it all make sense: We are declared to be right in God's eyes, not because of our own works or merits, but solely because of God's gracious favor towards us, on account of Christ, which we receive through faith alone.

The words "before God" should not escape our attention. What Christianity is "all about," before it is about anything else, is addressing our deepest, most fundamental problem. The doctrine of justification addresses the "problem of God," the "Problem that *is* God."

The "God-Problem"

As sinners, our most pressing problem is the problem of the God who demands perfection, perfect righteousness. That we are not perfect, that we cannot live perfect lives, because of our sin, is a real problem—not for God of course, but for us, since God, who is perfectly just, is angry because of our sin and punishes it.

Justification is the solution to the "God-Problem."

Christianity stands for a lot, indeed. It stands for personal and psychological wholeness. It stands for fairness and justice. It stands for peace and the promotion of a godly life. It stands for the poor and the widows and the downtrodden. But before it is any of these things, it is about the proclamation of the Good News that God Himself has, solely by His grace, in Christ, apart from our works, solved our most serious problem: *God Himself!*

All is right with *God!* What a beautiful doctrine! This gives Christ all the glory for His wonderful work of saving sinners; but it also gives us, sinners, the maximum amount of comfort possible. Apart from our works, by grace, on account of Christ, through faith—these are the four "component parts" of what is known as the "doctrine of justification." Right here is the heart and core of what "we believe, teach and confess."

Apart from Works

Imagining that we are saved by our works is perhaps the greatest, and most dangerous, theological error there is.

Paul makes it very clear that we are not saved on account of any works of ours. "For all have sinned and fall short of the glory of God," he writes (Rom. 3:23). We might, perhaps, be able to justify ourselves if we could live a life pleasing and acceptable to God. But, as Paul says, we have sinned, every one of us, and the wages for our sin is death (Rom. 6:23), spiritual and eternal death.

By attempting to make ourselves right in God's eyes with our own sinful efforts, we only dig ourselves deeper into a pit. We only make things worse for ourselves. This is what Paul means when he says that the Law increases sin (Rom. 3:20). When we view ourselves from the perspective of God's perfect Law, we see only how sinful and unworthy we are. The Law, in this sense, serves as sort of a mirror. It points out our great sinfulness and deprives us of any basis for making a claim upon God, any basis for boasting (Rom. 3:27; Eph. 2:9).

With nowhere else to look, we are forced to look outside of ourselves for the solution to our Problem. When we do this, the Law has served its purpose. It drives us to God.

In short, the first part of the doctrine of justification is sort of a negative statement—negative about ourselves, that is. It tells us what our justification is not: It is not due to our works, our merits, what we say or do or are; not due to anything in us. Rather it is due to something outside of ourselves—to the grace of God alone.

Which brings us to the second part of our doctrine.

By Grace

If we are not saved on the basis of our own efforts, then on what basis are we saved? On the basis of the grace of God.

Few teachings are more clear in Scripture than this. The entire history of God's people in the Old Testament is really the story of human sin and divine grace. This is perhaps nowhere more clear than in the wonderful miracle of grace that occurs in Gen. 12:1.

After a "gracious" creating in Genesis 1 and 2, the story of God's creatures, especially His human creatures, is really the story of a most ungracious falling away: The Fall into sin; Cain kills his brother, Abel; the Flood as punishment for great evil; the Tower of Babel; and so forth. Then, in Genesis 12, there occurs the greatest miracle of salvation. From all the mass of sinful humanity, God chooses for Himself one, Abram, whom He will bless by making him the father of a great nation, in whom all the nations of the world will be blessed (Gen. 12:2–3).

The New Testament continues the story of the Old, the story of human sin and divine grace, culminating in the arrival of "grace incarnate," our Lord Jesus Christ, into a world darkened by sin. In Him and from His fullness, God showered upon humanity "grace upon grace" (John 1:16). It is a "gift of His grace" (Eph. 2:8), nothing in us. God now looks favorably upon us; He favors us with His countenance (Num. 6:25); His face smiles upon us. Why? That is the third part of the doctrine of justification.

For Christ's Sake

That God should view us in such a favorable way is due alone to the fact that Jesus Christ, God's own Son, took our place and fulfilled the Law in our place.

Jesus is God's Divine Remedy for human sin. In His perfect life and perfect suffering and death, He took upon Himself the sins of the entire world, so that we might be presented to the Father perfect and without spot or blemish. This is the message of the entire Bible: That God Himself has solved the problem of our sinfulness and our sins in Jesus Christ. What a great mystery: God the "Problem," has, in Christ, become God the Solution.

But who is this Jesus? This is an important question, since who we think Jesus is will determine in some important ways what we look to Him for.

Jesus Himself thought this was an important question when He asked His disciples, "Who do you say I am?" (Matt. 16:15). Peter's answer, given for all the disciples, has become the normative response: "You are the Christ, the Son of the living God."

Jesus of Nazareth is the Son of God; He is both man, born of Mary, and God, conceived by the Holy Spirit. Upon this confession, Christ has built His church in such a way that even the gates of hell cannot prevail against it (Matt. 16:18).

This is what Christianity is first and most fundamentally about: It is about Jesus, the God-Man, the Savior of the world. With this confession upon its lips, the Church of Jesus Christ entered into history. And with these words on its lips, "Jesus Christ is Lord" (Phil. 2:11), the Church will pass from time and enter into eternity.

But we're still stuck in time, this particular time. So, how is it that what Jesus was and did back then and over there becomes what He is and does for me here and now? Well, that's part four of our definition.

Through Faith

Who Jesus was and what He did 2,000 years ago *for the world* becomes what He is and does *for us* today through faith. By faith alone, we apprehend, we receive, the saving blessings that Jesus lived and died to secure for us.

By faith alone. But what does this mean? Many think that faith is that part of the salvation process that is left to us. "All we have to do is believe." "We can only accept the gift offered." "We only decide to believe; we have to make a decision." These and many other kinds of statements that we hear very often betray some of the misunderstandings that surround much talk of faith: That it's our part of salvation. God has His part and we have ours.

This is not what the Bible means when it speaks of faith. When Paul says that we are saved by faith (Rom. 3:21; Eph. 2:8), he is not saying that we are saved by something we do, but rather precisely by something that we do *not* do. Faith saves because of its Object, our Lord Jesus Christ and His perfect works and merits. To speak of salvation "through faith" is the same as to speak of it "apart from works." Both of these statements are designed to deflect attention away from ourselves, our merits and works, and to direct it to Christ. In the Bible, faith talk is Christ talk.

That is why it has become customary for theologians and pastors to speak of faith as a means, an "instrument," *through which* we receive the saving gifts of Christ. So, faith is "trust in the heart of the believer," through which he or she is given the grace of God. In fact, even faith itself "is a gift of His grace" (Eph. 2:8). Christ alone gets the glory when a sinner is saved.

And the sinner? We get the maximum comfort possible, for our salvation rests alone on the firm Foundation of Jesus Christ.

So What?

Theology, in a way, consists in answering two simple questions. First, "what?" What does the Word of God say? What is the doctrine of justification? We have answered this question briefly here. But we have not finished until we have answered the second question: "So what?" So, what does it mean? What are the implications of the doctrine of justification?

Well, so what? So what does it mean that we are justified before God apart from works of the Law, by grace, on account of Christ, through faith? What does it mean that our greatest Problem has been solved?

Literally, it means everything to us. Having been declared by the Gospel to be righteous before God, there opens up to us a whole new reality, a reality lived through faith in Christ. As Paul says, "Therefore, if anyone is in Christ, he is a new creation; the old has gone, the new has come!" (2 Cor. 5:17).

To live in this new way—by faith in Christ—means that the Christian no longer lives in himself or herself. The call of the Gospel is, in a sense, a call to live outside of ourselves: We live in Christ through faith and in our neighbor through love. The call of the Gospel is the call to freedom, freedom from the confines of our old—*from* our old—self-serving way of life.

The doctrine of justification means that we no longer live in the old way, selfishly hoarding our good works for our own benefit. In fact, we know now that we do not need our good works to earn God's favor. We already have, through faith, the perfect good works of Jesus as our own. In God's eyes, we are already perfect, even as our Lord is perfect. No, we don't need our good works for ourselves any longer, so we are free to give our good works away to our neighbor, who does, sometimes desperately, need them.

That's what the Gospel of the justification of sinners by grace through faith in Jesus Christ does for us. It calls us to live outside of ourselves; calls us to live in Christ through faith and to live in our neighbors through love.

That's what it's all about.

FOR REFLECTION

1. What are the different ways people search for meaning and fulfillment in today's world?

2. Why is "imagining we are saved by works . . . perhaps the greatest, and most dangerous, theological error"? In what ways do Christians often "fall prey" to an attitude of works-righteousness?

3. Read Romans 3:21–28. How is God's righteousness made known to the world (v. 21)? How does it become ours (v. 28)? In what way is boasting "excluded" by faith (v. 27)?

4. How does the truth of justification "by grace, for Christ's sake, through faith" answer the question "So what?" What does justification mean for your relationships? your work and priorities?

5. How would you respond to the statement, "If you want to be a Christian, you must give up . . . ?"

FOR FURTHER READING

- Romans 4:1–25
- Luther's *Small Catechism,* The Third Article
- David Benke, God's Laws Don't Have Loopholes (CPH, 1995)

THE MEANS OF GRACE
(ARTICLE 5)

Richard G. Kapfer

> The Lord is always there for us. We know this, not because we can look
> inside ourselves for assurance, but because we can look outside to Him
> in His powerful, objective, certain Word of promise and life.

Bowling Alone: That's the title of a book that tries to describe the
sense of isolation in much of contemporary American life. The author
states that bowling-alley owners are seeing an increasing number of people who come in alone and *bowl alone.*

People also are less inclined to join groups—whether service clubs,
social clubs or civic organizations. And, this carries over to the reluc-
tance of many people to do much more than *attend* a church, but not to
join.

Why? Busy schedules, single-parent households, lack of trust toward
others, even some jobs that don't require leaving the house—and a growing isolation as a result.

There are many people today who live spiritually as though they can
"bowl alone" in their relationship with God. Some, for example, believe
that God is found, accepted and worshiped by looking within—and stay-
ing focused within. Proponents of "New Age" religions claim that God is
within us, so if we look within, we'll find God!

It's not a great step to go from this claim to the claim that each person
is God and thus is answerable only to himself or herself. The source of
truth, of spiritual wisdom, of ethics, of making choices is found within
oneself and can change as society or one's opinion changes.

Many people resemble the people of Luther's time who are described
in Article 5 of the Augsburg Confession, "who think that the Holy Spirit
comes to men without the external Word through their own preparations
and works."

Some churches apparently find the Holy Spirit's "tools" of Word and
Sacrament to be pretty mundane and unexciting—given perhaps for less-
er Christians, but not for those who have reached a higher consciousness
or appreciation for God! At first glance it seems that they have latched
onto a more dramatic and "relevant" walk with God—until they begin to
discuss what this means in terms of the grace of God and the work of the
Spirit. *They* are in charge, they think. They don't need what God gives.
They can go it alone.

It's not unusual to observe certain Lutherans who've decide to go it
alone. They're the ones who long ago packed their confirmation-instruc-

tion books in a box holding other discarded things from their childhoods. They assumed that, having been confirmed, they had had enough religion to get by for the rest of their lives. Only later in life, if ever, do they realize that something is missing, and the hollow spot is in the depths of their souls.

Filling the Void

The problem with "bowling alone" spiritually is that by ourselves and on our own, all that we really have is emptiness. That emptiness may at times be temporarily filled with emotionalism, but when the emotion, the subjective feelings, the fleeting happiness is gone—and it *will* be swiftly gone—then the emptiness returns and seems even more empty and hopeless, which it is.

Our God knows us! After all, in His Son He lived among us! He knows we can't go it alone. That's why Jesus promised the Comforter, the Holy Spirit, to His followers (John 14:26). No depending upon "inner voices," emotionally charged experiences, or subjective wishes and longings. Not for His loved ones! Instead, He comes through the powerful, objective, stand-by-itself, for-certain Word of the Gospel—read on a page, heard in a sermon, shared by even the humblest believer. And He comes through and in the Sacraments—Holy Baptism's water and the Word: "Baptize . . . in the name"; and Holy Communion's bread and wine/body and blood and the Word: "This is . . . for you."

These are the *means*, the *channels*, the *instruments* that the Holy Spirit uses to bestow upon us the forgiving, justifying, refreshing, empowering grace of God.

The voice of the pastor may be flat and dull, or exciting and engaging; the place where he preaches may be humble or magnificent; the baptismal water may be taken from a tiny bowl or a crashing ocean surf; the bread and wine may be served from a paten and chalice made of gold or of paper. No matter. These serve the Holy Spirit's gifts. Hearts are touched. Lives are reversed. Attitudes and opinions are changed. Sin is washed away. Hope is given. Life is bestowed.

The Ministry and the Means of Grace

"To obtain such faith God instituted the office of the ministry, that is, provided the Gospel and the sacraments." There is a mission thrust in these words. As one writer has put it, Article 5 "must be seen as the foundational platform on which both the royal priesthood and the office of called pastor rest under Christ's mandate for carrying His Word to the world." This involves the mission of the Church under the Spirit to speak and live and celebrate and share the Good News that God for Jesus' sake has reconciled all sinners to Himself, taking their sins from them and placing them on His Son. This is nothing more or less than taking seriously the fact that, through the sharing of the Gospel, the Holy Spirit works faith.

The ministry of the Gospel includes knowing and believing that the Gospel is "the power of God for the salvation of everyone who believes" (Rom. 1:16). Sin may have torn lives apart and caused everyone involved to despair of a solution. Yet because of the Gospel's power in the resurrection of Jesus Christ and His victory over sin and death, we, too, can conquer our own little deaths. This is the Spirit's power for a Nicodemus who had to "be born again," and for an adulterous woman who thirsted for living water from out of a parched and dead-end life, and for a Simon Peter who swore that he didn't even know the Lord Jesus, and for you and me when we can only beg for the Lord's grace and mercy.

The wonder is that the Lord is always there to help, especially in time of need. And we know this, not because we are able to look inside ourselves for assurance, but because we can look outside our otherwise pinched selves to Him in His powerful, objective, certain Word of promise and life!

We surely don't need to go it alone. As part of His ordinance and plan, the same Lord Jesus Christ who saved us and sent the Holy Spirit also established the distinctive office of the public ministry. These "gifts" to the church are called by the Lord Himself into the holy ministry in order to be instruments in the hands of the Holy Spirit to equip and build up the royal priests of God through Word and Sacraments. Their task is a holy task. Their ministry is the one assigned by the Lord Himself. They are called "not to preach ourselves, but Jesus Christ as Lord, and ourselves as your servants for Jesus' sake" (2 Cor. 4:5).

And all this because "through these, as through means, he gives the Holy Spirit, who works faith, when and where he pleases, in those who hear the Gospel." Underscoring all of this is the certainty of our salvation—not because we think so, feel it's so, or imagine it to be so, but because it *is* so.

God Himself says so!

FOR REFLECTION

1. What evidence of "bowling alone" do you find in the world around you? When do we try to "bowl alone" in our spiritual lives?

2. Why might people think the Word and sacraments are "mundane and unexciting"? Why is it always a temptation to "look inside ourselves" for assurance in times of doubts and troubles?

3. Read 1 Corinthians 12:1–11, 27–30. Relate the ministry of Word and sacrament to St. Paul's teaching on the body of Christ.

4. In what ways is a pastor's ministry different from the lay Christian's calling? In what ways are these two callings similar?

5. The Holy Spirit, Martin Luther writes, "calls, gathers, enlightens, and sanctifies the whole Christian church on earth, and keeps it with Jesus Christ in the one true faith." What are God's blessings of "life together" in a Christian congregation? In what ways does fellowship in Christ strengthen your faith and daily witness?

FOR FURTHER READING

- Acts 2:1–47
- Luther's *Small Catechism*, Holy Baptism and The Sacrament of the Altar

THE NEW OBEDIENCE (ARTICLES 6 AND 20)

Francis C. Rossow

If we're not saved by doing good works, why bother?

At the time of Martin Luther, one supporter of the Reformation became so enthusiastic about the Biblical truth that good works don't save people that he claimed, "Good works are harmful to salvation."

Not only was his assertion logically wrong, it was, above all, theologically wrong. Article 4 of the Formula of Concord corrected this error.

Few today are so negative toward good works. But our attitude toward good works still may not be all that it should be. We may feel uneasy when we hear a pastor or teacher encourage good works; we may think it's "un-Lutheran" for them to do so. Or we ourselves may keep silent about good works for fear that people might misunderstand any such talk as "moralizing" or implying that they help toward our eternal salvation. We may conclude that since good works don't save us, they are, therefore, comparatively unimportant in the plan of God.

In short, we may tolerate good works, but demote them to second-class citizens.

The Augsburg Confession addresses this problem. Article 6 says "that it is necessary to do the good works commanded by God. We must do so because it is God's will and not because we rely on such works to merit justification before God." Article 20 says, "Our teachers teach in addition that it is necessary to do good works, not that we should trust to merit grace by them but because it is the will of God."

The Will of God

Indeed, doing good works is the will of God. Not only is it the will of God that all people be saved (1 Tim. 2:4), it is also His will "that you should be holy" (1 Thess. 4:3). The writer to the Hebrews prays that "the God of peace . . . make you perfect in every good work to do his will, working in you that which is well-pleasing in his sight" (13:21 KJV).

Paul's words in Titus 2:14 suggest that Christ came to our world for two reasons: (1) to save us ("to redeem us from all wickedness"), and (2) to make us good people ("to purify for himself a people that are his very own, eager to do what is good").

Because of Christ's saving life, death and resurrection, God does two things to us:

(1) He *declares* us righteous through Christ; and,

(2) He *begins to make* us righteous through Christ.

We need to keep both of these activities of God in mind. Likewise, we need to see both of them in proper relationship to each other. It is to this relationship that we now turn.

Often the Scriptures divide the question (as above), presenting God's work as if it were two activities: (1) declaring us righteous through Christ; and, (2) beginning to make us righteous through Christ. The Scriptures do this because they want to make it unmistakably clear that the second activity has no bearing on the first; God's making us righteous has no influence on His declaring us righteous.

Not only are we not saved by our own good works, we are not even saved by the good works God Himself manufactures in us. Our salvation is 100 percent complete and certain the moment God declares us righteous on account of Christ. We're in. God's saying it's so makes it so.

The best example of this in the Bible is the thief on the cross. With his sordid past staring him in the face and death but a few moments away, having absolutely nothing going for him, he threw himself onto the mercy of the One on the middle cross, Jesus. And Jesus said to him, "I tell you the truth, today you will be with me in paradise" (Luke 23:43).

That our eternal salvation is entirely the doing of God through Jesus, and that we contribute absolutely nothing toward it, is more than a correct doctrine—it's a comforting doctrine. Says Article 20: "God-fearing and anxious consciences find by experience that it [this doctrine] offers the greatest consolation because the consciences of men cannot be pacified by any work but only by faith when they are sure that for Christ's sake they have a gracious God."

Oh, what a relief it is! Even the best of us (so called) don't have to fret over whether we've been good enough for God. And even the worst of us (again, so called) can count on the same mercy of God through Jesus available to all other people.

Faith and Works Together

But sometimes the Scriptures reassemble the question; they "put Humpty-Dumpty back together again." They present God's work of declaring us righteous and beginning to make us righteous as if this work were one activity. They do so because they want to make it unmistakably clear that God's work is one, even as He is one—that declaring us righteous and beginning to make us righteous are really only two aspects of one plan, two sides of the same coin.

Faith and works are a unity, as James repeatedly reminds us in his letter; you can't have one without the other. Faith and works go together—like bread and butter, love and marriage, horse and carriage, a ship and its wake, Rosencrantz and Guildenstern, Tweeledum and

Tweedledee. When God declares us righteous through Christ, He at the same time begins to make us righteous through Christ—even though the second part of the activity has no bearing on the first.

An interesting instance of this unity between faith and works, "justification" and "sanctification," occurs in Rom. 10:9-10. Here, Paul not only speaks of a justification aspect (believing with the heart) and a sanctification aspect (confessing with the mouth) in one and the same breath, but he begins in v. 9 with an "un-Lutheran" order, mentioning the sanctification aspect first and the justification aspect second, seemingly putting the cart before the horse, the result before the cause! Then in v. 10 Paul reverses the order, returning (perhaps to the relief of some of us) to the traditional sequence. Rather than see in this passage a careless or inconsistent arrangement of items, I prefer to see implied the unity of justification and sanctification. Where the one is, the other is.

Consider the term "redemption." To "redeem" means to buy back, a piece of property perhaps (like a field, for example), and usually at a staggering price. But why does a person buy a field? To save it? Yes. But in the long run, a person buys a field in order that he might clear it of litter and refuse, cultivate it, and make it bear fruit, yield a crop. So God has "redeemed" us, bought us back, paying the staggering price of His Son's execution and damnation. Why? To save us, of course. But more: so that He might clear us of litter and refuse, cultivate us, and make us bear fruit. The unity of salvation and Christian living is implicit in the redemption metaphor.

The clearest Biblical evidence for the unity of faith and good works is Ephesians 2:8–10, a passage that divides the question even as it assembles it, and vice-versa. Verses 8 and 9 tell us so clearly that good works have nothing to do with salvation: "For it is by grace you have been saved through faith—and this not from yourselves, it is the gift of God—not by works, so that no one can boast." But we Lutherans mustn't stop there. For right away comes v. 10, in which Paul restores good works to a position of prominence—not in the area of salvation, no, but in the area of everyday Christian living. "For we are God's workmanship, created in Christ Jesus to do good works, which God prepared in advance for us to do."

It isn't just our salvation that God planned way back in eternity (Eph. 1:4). We learn from v. 10 that God also planned our good works way back in eternity. Clearly, God thinks them important.

And that's the point. God think good works important. So should we. Recognizing the unity of faith and works, their inseparableness, will help us do that. No longer will we regard good works as something tacked on: an afterthought, an addendum, a footnote. Rather, they belong. They're a part of God's eternal agenda.

The faith and works that God so often joins together in His Word, we must not consistently put asunder. We put them asunder only—as the Bible does—when we discuss the question of how we are saved. But we hasten to put them back together again whenever we consider what God wants from us in our everyday living.

How Do We Do Good Works?

Given their importance, how do we do good works? To do good works we need the Gospel, the message of Christ crucified and risen. And we need that Gospel power every bit as much for Christian living as we need it for salvation. We are saved "by grace alone." We do good works "by grace alone."

All is of God through Jesus Christ. "I am the vine; you are the branches. If a man remains in me and I in him, he will bear much fruit; apart from me you can do nothing" (John 15:5). ". . . For it is God who works in you to will and to act according to his good purpose" (Phil. 2:13). "I can do everything through him who gives me strength" (Phil. 4:13). "Therefore, if anyone is in Christ, he is a new creation" (2 Cor. 5:17).

True, the Confessions often speak of faith as the power for good works. That's because faith is the receptacle for that power of God which manufactures good works. Faith then transmits that power. Says Article 20: "And because through faith the Holy Spirit is received, hearts are so renewed and endowed with new affections as to be able to bring forth good works."

But, ultimately, it is the power of God that is operative—not the power of faith. Faith, itself, in fact, is a product of God's manufacture. We are not saved *by* faith but rather *through* faith— by God's power through faith.

Picture faith and good works, justification and sanctification, as the two blades of a scissors. Call the top blade "faith," if you will, and the bottom blade "good works." Faith and works are two different realities, often apart from each other, even as there are two different blades of a scissors, often with a distance between them. But look again. The two blades of the scissors are ultimately one entity, for they are joined together at the axis, or handle, and most of the time work together as a unit. Even more to the purpose, realize that the power for either blade lies not in itself but in the hand that operates the handle.

So it is with faith and works. Whether functioning apart (as in the area of salvation) or functioning together (as in the area of everyday living), it is God's hand through Christ that supplies the power.

FOR REFLECTION

1. What is "the New Obedience"? Why are Christians often reluctant to talk about "Faith and Good Works"?

2. How has God "declared us righteous"? How does God "begin to make us righteous"? Why is it wrong to separate these two works of God?

3. Read John 15:1–8. How does the imagery of vine, gardener, and branches reveal God's will and work among His chosen people in Christ?

4. In what ways does Christ's Word and sacrament renew and strengthen you in daily life?

5. How does your congregational fellowship in Christ help you to live and witness in today's world?

FOR FURTHER READING

- Hebrews 10:19–39
- Luther's *Small Catechism*, Table of Duties

THE HOLY CHRISTIAN CHURCH (ARTICLES 7 AND 8)

Eugene F. Klug

There is more to "church" than you might imagine.

What comes to mind when you hear the word "church"?

Some of us may think back to the time, years ago, when the bells at the church down the street pealed loudly. Our parents probably told us they were saying, "Come to church."

In many homes, mother was rousing her youngsters with the firm reminder, "It's Sunday; time to get up for church." The response wasn't always "Oh, goody, what should I wear?" but just as likely, "Do we have to? I'm tired and wanna sleep some more." Maybe even Mom and Dad struggled with the temptation to do something else for a change—the spirit being willing (sort of), but the flesh, oh, so weak.

Nonetheless, church was a real part of life.

It even followed you into military service. There were divine worship services even at sea. "Church call" would go out over the ship's intercom, "Divine services are now being held on the foc'sle, the smoking lamp is out, keep silence about the decks." Except for those conducting essential operations, men were generally free to "go to church."

Troops on the ground were ordinarily not forgotten, either. Intrepid chaplains, even in forward areas, would pass the word for ad hoc church services in make-shift worship settings, with preached word and prayers, perhaps hymns, maybe even the Lord's Supper, circumstances permitting.

Mention the word "church," Martin Luther observed even in his day, "and the common man thinks of the stone house called 'church'"—pretty much in the same way as many of us look back to the bells of the neighborhood church sounding out their "church call" to come to worship.

Luther is not faulting such thoughts. After all, strong stone and brick churches were emblematic of the firm foundation on which people's faith in Christ was based. But he points out how, over the years, the term "church" had become somewhat ill-defined, even distorted. We, therefore, need to dig deeper if we want to get at "what, who and where the church is."

The Church Is People

A major treatise of Luther's, "On the Councils and the Church," appeared in 1539. There, Luther devoted himself to pinpointing precisely the true nature of the church, directing us back to the Apostles' Creed, which "clearly indicates what the church is, namely, a communion of saints," a fellowship of people "who believe in Christ."

This definition runs throughout his writings, that the church is the total company of believers built upon Christ, against which not even the gates of hell will prevail (Matt. 16:18). The church comprises the "members of God's household" (Eph. 2:19), which transcends all space and time and constitutes the followers of Christ to be "fellow citizens with God's people"—the "saints," says the King James Version—in heaven.

We are in this company of believers. So are the patriarchs, like Abraham, all the way back to Adam, as well as others still to be gathered till the end of time here on earth.

These are the total company of believers built upon Christ: the holy Christian church.

The year 1530 marked one of Christendom's historic moments, as the Protestant party, accused of heresy, defended itself at the imperial Diet of Augsburg. Organizational structures, ceremonies, religious rules and dress, pontifical power and edifice did not constitute the church, they asserted. Rather, referencing the Bible, they said in the Augsburg Confession that "the Christian church, properly speaking, is nothing else than the assembly of all believers and saints" (AC 7); also, that this "one holy Christian church will be and remain forever" (AC 8).

The confessors, clearly supported by Holy Scripture, had struck a decisive blow for the true nature of the church as "the assembly of all believers among whom the Gospel is preached in its purity and the holy sacraments are administered according to the Gospel."

Luther could not go to Augsburg for this crucial gathering of political bigwigs and sundry ecclesiastical figures. But the *Large and Small Catechisms* had come from Luther's pen in 1529, and the Lutheran confessors had these and other documents with them at Augsburg.

In the *Large Catechism,* Luther had written concerning the church: "[It is] a unique community in the world . . . , the mother that begets and bears every Christian through the Word of God." He had further explained that "the creed calls the holy Christian church a *communio sanctorum,* 'a communion of saints'" and that "both expressions have the same meaning."

This "little holy flock or community of pure saints under one head, Christ, . . . is called together by the Holy Spirit in one faith, mind, and understanding." Luther expressed it in very personal terms to which we, too, can resonate: "I was brought to it by the Holy Spirit and incorporated into it through the fact that I have heard and still hear God's Word, which is the first step in entering it." And though we remain sinners till we die, "everything in the Christian church is so ordered that we may daily obtain full forgiveness of sins through the Word and the signs [sacraments] appointed to comfort and revive our consciences as long as we live" (LC 2, 47ff.).

The church is no mere theoretical concept, but a very real, existential, true-to-life fact in this world. Indeed, this household of faith, or fellowship of believers, built upon Christ reaches also into heaven. But it is first of all right here on earth, for wherever the Word is, there God builds His church, and He promises that the preaching of His Word will never be in vain but will bear fruit (Is. 55:11; Acts 2:37–42; 10:43).

Thus there is one, united entity—"a holy Christian people."

The Congregation

As we see from the frequent references in the New Testament, this entity includes the local gathering of confessing believers into congregations—in Corinth, Rome and Ephesus, for example. But always around the Word! So, Scripture very definitely denominates these, too, as "church," for believers built upon Christ are present there and they confess their faith, pray and worship, and seek to bring forth the fruits of faith with godly living.

The Greek term used in the New Testament (nearly 100 times!) for such local entities of believers is *ekklesia,* which in English simply translates as assembly, congregation or church.

It is entirely possible, as we learn from the story of Ananias and Sapphira (Acts 5), for unbelievers or hypocrites to become connected with this fellowship (the "visible church"), be baptized, profess the Christian faith, even hold church office, all the while covering up their unbelief. Article 8 of Augsburg notes that "in this life many false Christians, hypocrites, and even open sinners remain among the godly." But by virtue of the genuine believers gathered around the Word, it is still properly identified as a Christian church, and thus also co-extensive with the one, holy Christian church confessed in the Creed.

Jesus cautioned His disciples, and so also us today, against trying to sift the tares from the wheat (Matthew 13). We can't look into people's hearts as He can. Manifest, unrepentant sinners, of course, are to be disciplined in proper manner, however, as Christ explained in Matt. 18:15-20. The hope is to bring them to repentance.

Unity and Division

Article 7 of the Confession expresses the church's responsibility under God that "the Gospel is preached in its purity and the holy sacraments are administered according to the Gospel."

The true unity of the church thus is to be grounded upon orthodox teaching, the teaching of the Bible. This is the will of God. The spirit of compromise, which reduces or rejects what God has taught in His Word, breeds indifference toward error and eventually may endanger the salvation of souls. God does not sanction diversity in doctrine. To countenance it or to practice church fellowship—to practice what we often call "unionism"—with those who stray from the Bible's teaching does not advance the cause of the Gospel or serve true unity in the church, but stands opposed to the spirit of truth.

Equally contrary to God's will, though, is the spirit of separatism that causes division in the church. Article 7 adds: "It is not necessary for the true unity of the Christian church that ceremonies, instituted by men, should be observed uniformly in all places." In matters not fixed by Scripture there can be various usages allowable within the bounds of Christian liberty and, therefore, not in themselves wrong even though different from those practiced elsewhere.

Divisiveness for which there is no justifiable basis is sinful. It may even parade under the cloak of concern for purity of doctrine, while in fact it emanates from a spirit of malice and sinful pride, giving rise to partyism, power-scrambling, feuds and personality-cults.

The apostle Paul was greatly concerned when divisions broke out in the Corinthian church, causing great harm to the peace and unity of the congregation. In strong terms he exhorted: "I appeal to you, brothers, in the name of our Lord Jesus Christ, that all of you agree with one another so that there may be no divisions among you and that you may be perfectly united in mind and thought" (1 Cor. 1:10).

A "Chosen People"

The great prerogatives that the bride of Christ, the holy Christian church, possesses are the keys of the kingdom of heaven, the Word, Baptism and the Sacrament of the Altar—God's designated instruments for the nurture and care of His sheep, the believers. This is a high trust, a truly wonderful, unique, sovereign trust from God.

The apostle Peter pinpoints it when he writes to the churches scattered throughout Asia Minor: "But you are a chosen people, a royal priesthood, a holy nation, a people belonging to God, that you may declare the praises of him who called you out of darkness into his wonderful light" (1 Pet. 2:9).

So, the word "church" is used in several senses. The "Explanation" of the *Small Catechism,* used in many confirmation classes, tells us that basically "the holy Christian church is the communion of saints, the total number of those who believe in Christ." It adds that the word "church" is also used to indicate the visible church of God, a denomination, a local congregation, and a house of worship.

Finally, the "Explanation" also tells us what the Bible teaches about our life in the church; namely, that:

- "We should seek always to be and remain members of the invisible church, Christ's body, by sincere faith in Christ, our Savior";
- "We should be faithful to that visible church, or denomination, which professes and teaches all of the Bible's doctrines purely and administers the sacraments according to Christ's institution";
- "We should avoid false teachers, false churches, and all organizations that promote a religion that is contrary to God's Word"; and
- "We should maintain and extend God's church by telling others about Jesus Christ, by personal service, and by prayer and financial support."

FOR REFLECTION

1. How have traditional ideas about the church changed in the past 25 years? How have expectations of the church changed?

2. In what ways is the Christian church "visible"? In what ways is the Church "invisible"?

3. Read Ephesians 4:1–16. How does St. Paul portray the Church's unity? How does he describe the Church's purpose?

4. What are the dangers of compromise in the Church? What are the dangers of rigidity in our mission and ministry?

5. What comfort do you have in knowing that the church will "be and remain forever"?

FOR FURTHER READING

- Ephesians 3:1–21
- Luther's *Small Catechism*, Third Article and Explanation

GOD'S WORK IN BAPTISM (ARTICLE 9)

Jerald C. Joersz

God baptizes us, giving us new birth and the hope of eternal life.

"When God speaks about a splinter," Luther wrote, "His Word makes the splinter as important as the sun."

The same can be said of the water of Holy Baptism. God reaches down into the ordinary, takes water and enwraps it with His Word of command and promise. Just as God entered human flesh in Jesus Christ, who "lived for a while among us" (John 1:14), so God takes simple water and through His Word becomes present in it.

Baptism "is not simply a natural water, but a divine heavenly, holy, and blessed water—praise it in any other terms you can—all by virtue of the Word, which is a heavenly, holy Word which no one can sufficiently extol, for it contains all the fullness of God," is the way it's put in the *Large Catechism* (LC 4, 17).

"A cow or a dog sees only water," Luther once wrote, but "the pious see and appreciate the Word in the water."

Thus, Baptism for Christians "is a treasure greater and nobler than heaven and earth," the *Large Catechism* explains (LC 4, 10).

And why is Baptism such a noble thing? Because, as the Catechism says, it is *God's* work: "To be baptized in God's name is to be baptized not by men but by God himself" (LC 4, 10).

If this is all true, then why the seemingly lackadaisical attitude of some today toward Baptism? Not even the prodding of Grandma "to have it done" can move some to bring their children to Baptism!

And what about Christians for whom Baptism is rarely a point of reference, to say nothing of it being the daily source of strength and encouragement for a new life?

Could it be that lurking beneath present-day attitudes is what one theologian today has called "the offense of externality"—baptism looks so ordinary, how can it do such great things?

God Is at Work

Maybe a "poof" of smoke, a flash of light, a roll of the drum would for some remove the offense. But the truth is that in a quiet, unassuming way, God is at work through plain water to do a mighty thing.

We need only look at what Baptism gives and offers to discover what a precious treasure Baptism is. According to Christ's command, the church baptizes "in [literally, 'into'] the name of the Father and of the Son and of the Holy Spirit" (Matt. 28:19). These "words of institution" teach that Baptism has God's name in it. When we are baptized, we are joined to His name, and thus to Him. Where God's name is, the *Large Catechism* teaches, "there must also be life and salvation" (LV 4, 27).

Baptism truly is "a washing of regeneration and renewal in the Holy Spirit . . . so that we might be justified by his grace and become heirs in hope of eternal life" (Titus 3:5,7). Again, St. Paul writes to the Galatians, "For as many of you as were baptized into Christ have put on Christ." This means we are forgiven and thus children of God (Gal. 3:24-27).

Christians, therefore, need not flinch from saying forthrightly, *"Baptism saves."* This is exactly how the Bible puts it: "He [God] *saved us . . . by the washing of regeneration"* (Titus 3:5; see 1 Peter 3:21).

Baptism saves because through it we are united with Christ, who alone is our Savior (Rom. 6:4). Consider the boldness of Luther's language: "Through Baptism [a person] is bathed in the blood of Christ and cleansed from sins." Where there is forgiveness of sins, the *Small Catechism* affirms, "there is also life and salvation."

Someone may be led to ask, "Well, then, are you saying that Baptism works miracles?" Indeed it does. Without God's help, we are lost forever, under the power of sin (Rom. 1:9) and subject to death (Rom. 5:12). But God "delivered us from the dominion of darkness and transferred us to the kingdom of his beloved Son." This rescue happened long ago when Christ died and rose, but it happens *personally* to each of us at our Baptism!

In the *Large Catechism,* Luther concludes his discussion by declaring what "a great and excellent thing Baptism is." It "snatches us from the jaws of the devil and makes God our own, overcomes and takes away sin and daily strengthens the new man, always remains until we pass from this present misery to eternal glory" (LC 4, 83). Or, as the Augsburg Confession simply, yet powerfully, states, "Grace is offered through it" (AC 9).

Baptism is necessary for precisely this reason: In it, God graciously gives to us the forgiveness earned by His Son on the cross.

Baptism, therefore, is sheer Gospel. "Here in Baptism there is brought free to every man's door just such priceless medicine which swallows up death and saves the lives of all men," the *Large Catechism* affirms (LC 4, 43). Like the crossing of the Israelites through the Red Sea, a mighty deliverance takes place in the lives of those who are baptized.

We may sometimes wonder whatever happened to Baptism in the lives of some. They seem to have left the faith into which they were baptized. Sadly, this is far too often the case. But we should not conclude from this that something has gone wrong with their Baptism! Like a firmly anchored ship, it remains a means of rescue, even though someone may slip and fall overboard. If this has happened, says the *Large Catechism,* that person should be urged to "immediately head for the ship and cling to it until he can climb aboard again and sail on it as he had done before" (LC 4, 32).

Baptism for Daily Living

No event in the personal history of the Christian has greater significance for daily life than Baptism. In Baptism, "every Christian has enough to practice all his life," the *Large Catechism* tells us (LC 4, 41). This is because of what St. Paul says *happened,* and each day still *happens:* "We were buried therefore with him by baptism into death, so that as Christ was raised from the dead by the glory of the Father, we too might walk in newness of life" (Rom. 6:4).

At Baptism, we—our whole person, body and soul—were united with Christ, who died to sin and lives to God (Rom. 6:10). In our union with Christ, we reenact each day of our life exactly what took place at the baptismal font. We "put off the old nature" and "put on the new nature" (Eph. 4:22,24).

This activity the Lutheran Confessions refer to as daily repentance: "Repentance is really nothing else than baptism. What is repentance but an earnest attack on the old man and an entering upon a new life? If you live in repentance, therefore, you are walking in Baptism, which not only announces this new life but also produces, begins, and promotes it. . . ." (LC 4, 75).

This way of describing the Christian life is a far cry from the shallow moralizing talk we sometimes hear today, like, "There's a little bit of bad in the best of us and a little bit of good in the worst of us." Baptism spells *death*—death to the "old man" in us—and *life*—the rising of the "new man" "created after the likeness of God in true righteousness and holiness" (Eph. 4:24).

The old must die, and the new must daily come forth like a grain of wheat that falls into the ground to die, but to rise and bring forth fruit (see John 12:24).

Theologian Herbert Girgensohn put it graphically: "God does not feed the child who has fallen into the gutter with moral lectures on how he must behave himself. He lifts him out of the gutter and takes him into his house, the Father's house with its pure air of life and love that regulates the relationship of those who live in his household" *(Teaching Luther's Catechism,* Vol. 2, p. 24). As Girgensohn so rightly says, our new life in Christ is lived within God's family, the church (1 Cor. 12:13).

Faith and Infant Baptism

Many Christians are deeply troubled by the stress on Baptism as solely *God's* work, and ask where is *faith* in all of this?

It is just at this point that the church's historic practice of infant baptism comes up. "How can we baptize babies, when they can't believe?" goes the objection.

This is not a new question. In the Lutheran confessors' day, some even advocated the rebaptism of people baptized as infants because they considered a human response (e.g., confession of faith) necessary for a valid baptism ("Anabaptists" they were called). In response, Luther summarized well the nub of the problem in these words: "Everything depends upon the Word and commandment of God. . . . *For my faith does not constitute Baptism but receives it.* Baptism does not become invalid even if it is wrongly received or used, for it is bound not to our faith but to the Word" (LC 4, 53).

Faith receives the blessings of Baptism (whether present in adults or in children) and it is itself another miracle! Through the power of the Holy Spirit, the very faith that receives God's gifts is awakened or created (Titus 3:5), so that in the end it can be said, "He who believes and is baptized will be saved" (Mark 16:16).

Faith, in the Scriptural understanding, is not, so to speak, an independent act of a person who meets God half way—as two captains of a basketball team coming to center court to shake hands before the game begins. On the contrary, even though we do the believing, the whole initiative belongs to God, who in Christ Jesus accepts us. Faith, in a sense, is "being grasped" by the Lord's action. It's like our own birth. Apart from any decision on our part, we were conceived and born.

This is of enduring comfort to Christians, whose hope rests not in what they bring to Baptism, but in what God brings to them through it. Since this is so, Baptism remains throughout our lives a source of comfort and joy.

As the Apology of the Augsburg Confession says it, Baptism is a means through which God wants constantly to "admonish, cheer, comfort terrified minds to believe more firmly that their sins are forgiven" (Ap 4, 276). We can hardly think of a clearer testimony to the Reformation principle of "grace alone" than the practice of baptizing infants. "Baptism is not an act which we offer God but one in which God baptizes us through a minister functioning in his place," says the Apology (Ap 24, 18).

"To all appearances, it may not be worth a straw," wrote Luther of Baptism. But it is God's work, "fastened and enclosed with a jeweled clasp" (that is, the Word), and that makes it a thing of great dignity (LC 4, 8, 16).

Indeed, Baptism is as "important as the sun," and we pray that it will become a great and excellent thing also in our daily life.

FOR REFLECTION

1. Recall or share, if possible, a Baptism in your family.

Why was it so memorable?

2. Our "rescue happened long ago when Christ died and rose," the article notes, "but it happens personally to each of us at our Baptism". What does this mean? How does Romans 6:1–11 convey this important truth?

3. Read Colossians 2:6–12. What does Baptism mean for our daily life?

4. "In a quiet, unassuming way, God is at work through plain water to do a mighty thing." Why is it often difficult to accept this truth about Baptism? In what way is the "quiet, unassuming" character of Baptism like the incarnation?

5. How can we daily remember and celebrate God's gift of forgiveness in Baptism?

FOR FURTHER READING

- John 3:1–36
- Luther's *Small Catechism,* Baptism
- Richard A. Melheim, *Welcome to the Family!* (CPH, 1989)
- Harold Senkbeil, *Dying for Forgiveness* (CPH, 1994)

THE SACRAMENT OF THE ALTAR (ARTICLE 10)

Gregory Lockwood

In Holy Communion, Jesus Christ offers His very body and blood—and peace with God.

I remember how as a boy my eyes were drawn to the marble slab on the altar-face of our church, with the words lettered in gold: "Come unto me, all ye who labor and are heavy laden, and I will give you rest" (Matt. 11:28).

What those words must have meant to generations of weary men and women who came to that rural Australian church to be refreshed and find strength for another week!

Now the old wooden church has given way to a modern brick structure, and the marble slab has been removed to the entrance porch. But still it welcomes all who enter, beckoning them to the altar and the gifts offered there.

And it reminds us that the Sacrament of the Altar is not for those who think they are good and pure, with nothing on their consciences. Rather, it is for "those who labor and are heavy-laden with sin, fear of death, and the assaults of the flesh and the devil." So, says Martin Luther in the *Large Catechism,* "if you are heavy-laden and feel your weakness, go joyfully to the sacrament and receive refreshment, comfort and strength."

What kind of gifts are offered in the Holy Supper? Article 10 of the Augsburg Confession spells it out:

"It is taught among us that the true body and blood of Christ are really present in the Supper of the Lord under the form of bread and wine and are there distributed and received."

True Body, True Blood

These gifts—our Lord's true body and true blood—were His legacy to the Church on the night He was betrayed. They are His last will and testament, recorded in the words of institution in Matthew, Mark, Luke and First Corinthians.

The Reformer Martin Chemnitz writes: "The Son of God commended to His church the words of institution of the Supper in the form of a last will and testament—at a time of high emotion, with most fervent prayer, and under the most serious circumstances on the night in which He was betrayed. Therefore these words should be observed with the greatest reverence and piety and in the fear of the Lord by all people, for they are the words of the testament of the Son of God."

Sadly, wills often lead to heated arguments. Our Lord's last will and testament hasn't fared any better. Chemnitz comments: "Some evil genius has brought these most holy words into controversy." But, he continues, the solution is not to read into the words whatever we like. Rather, we should stick with "the simple, proper, and natural meaning."

And the Words of Institution are utterly simple: "This is my body, given for you. . . . This is my blood of the New Testament, shed for you for the forgiveness of sins."

But ever since our Lord instituted the Supper, people have found His words difficult and offensive. Human reason asks, "How can this man give us his flesh to eat?" (John 6:52). Was Jesus advocating cannibalism? So the pagan people of the Roman Empire concluded, thinking those perverse Christians engaged both in cannibalism and incest (after all, didn't they carry on about loving sisters and brothers?).

But it has not been only pagans who have misconstrued Jesus' words. Ever since the 11th century, there have been Christians who find His words offensive. Surely He couldn't have meant what He said! Surely His words must be understood symbolically: "This *represents* my body." For Christ's body has ascended into heaven. Now it's above the clouds; it cannot really be in the bread and wine on the altar. What we must do is lift up our hearts to Him in heaven and feed on Him by faith.

In Luther's Day, some reformers from Switzerland held this symbolic interpretation. On a Saturday afternoon in October 1529, the German Lutherans and the Swiss were gathered in the city of Marburg to debate the Lord's Supper and other issues. Afraid he might be tempted to compromise, Luther had written with chalk on the table, "This is my body," and then covered the words with the tablecloth. At a crucial point in the debate, he lifted the cloth and read the words, adding: "This is our Scripture passage. . . . I cannot pass over the text of my Lord Jesus Christ."

The body and blood we receive, of course, do not belong to a corpse, but to "the living bread who came down from heaven" (John 6:51). Just as the apostles heard Him, saw Him with their eyes, looked on Him and touched Him with their hands (1 John 1:1), so we are privileged to see and touch Him in the Lord's Supper.

The Word who became flesh for us remains true man. He is not a ghost. After His resurrection, Jesus invited the disciples, "Touch me and see, for a spirit doesn't have flesh and bones as you see me having" (Luke 24:39). And in the Supper, He gives us the same body once given on the cross, the same blood that was shed, but now wonderfully glorified by His ascension to the Father's right hand. It is the body and blood of the Lamb who stands victoriously, though He was slain, the Lamb of God who takes away the sin of the world (Rev. 5:6; John 1:29).

So the bread on the altar *is* the body of Christ; the wine in the cup *is* the blood of Christ. The speech Jesus uses is common in popular language. For example, we may point to a bottle of wine and say, "This is wine," or to a wallet and say, "This is money." Just as the dove that came down on Jesus at his baptism was the Holy Spirit (John 1:32), so the bread is the body, the wine is the blood.

So realistically do Lutherans understand Jesus' words that we believe even non-believers and unworthy Christians who present themselves at the Lord's Table receive His actual body and blood. "We hold that the bread and wine in the Supper are the true body and blood of Christ and that these are given and received not only by godly but also by wicked Christians," says the Smalcald Articles, another of our Lutheran Confessions. That is why St. Paul urges us to examine ourselves, lest we eat and drink to our detriment (1 Cor. 11:27–32).

The Augsburg Confession's article on the Lord's Supper is brief, because there was no difference between Lutherans and Catholics on the "real presence." Spelling out the Lutheran position more fully in the Apology of the Augsburg Confession, Reformer Philipp Melanchthon gladly states: "We know that not only the Roman Church affirms the bodily presence of Christ, but that the Greek Church has taken and still takes this position." The doctrine of the Real Presence was "the doctrine received in the whole church."

Some Unbiblical Notions

Because the Sacrament is pure Gospel offered to us by Christ, we cannot understand it as an "unbloody" sacrifice repeatedly offered by the church's priests, as does the Roman Catholic Church.

Nor do we believe that the bread is changed, or "transubstantiated," into the body of Christ (and the wine into His blood), so that it only *appears* to be bread. Scripture plainly teaches that "the bread which we break" is "the communion of the body of Christ" (1 Cor. 10:16). The bread is still bread, but "in, with and under" the bread we receive the body of Christ.

In recent times, the Sacrament has sometimes been treated frivolously by Christians who imagine that the meal mainly signifies good relationships on the horizontal level—communing with the pastor and one another. Christ is believed by them to be personally present, to be sure, but merely in a vague sense as the host or as another guest.

It is the vertical dimension—the communion with Christ's true body and blood—that is of crucial importance. For "the bread we break is the participation in the body of Christ; the cup of blessing is the participation in the blood of Christ" (1 Cor. 10:16). Only when the sacramental body and blood is properly appreciated and received ("in faith towards you"), does the Lord's Supper work to build us up on the horizontal level ("in fervent love toward one another").

The Benefits of the Supper

A post-communion prayer describes the chief blessings of the Supper as "pardon and peace": "O God the Father, . . . we thank you that . . . you have given us pardon and peace in this sacrament."

Our Lord's body was given, His blood poured out "for the forgiveness of sins" (Matt. 26:28). As the communion elements touch his lips, the believer is assured, "Your guilt is taken away, and your sin forgiven" (Is. 6:7). And, as the *Small Catechism* says, "where there is forgiveness of sins, there is also life and salvation."

At the end of another week, painfully conscious of how we've "daily sinned much and indeed deserve nothing but punishment," we approach the Lord's Table in joyful anticipation.

Dismissing other thoughts from our minds, we focus on the words, "Given and shed for you for the forgiveness of sins." Then, after receiving the body and blood, we leave the altar joyfully, with the words "Go in peace" ringing in our ears. Indeed, this sacrament is the Gospel.

Other benefits of the Supper may be listed briefly (following Martin Chemnitz):

- Here Christ lays hold on us (Phil. 3:12) as our true "flesh and blood" brother, joining us to Himself as intimately as possible;
- He comes to us in a very tangible way. The words "for you" assure us that God's forgiveness applies to each of us personally.
- In a wonderful way, His sinless body and blood begins to change us, sanctifying, restoring and blessing us in body and soul, "so that our depravity and misery are cured and renewed through the remedy of this most intimate union."
- By letting His glorified body and blood become part of our weak bodies, He assures us that our bodies will rise again on the last day.
- The Lord's Supper, celebrated "in remembrance of" Christ, is a powerful antidote against our forgetfulness and distraction. The Supper reminds us of what really matters.

Where Christians believe Christ's body and blood are actually there on the table, actually received by their lips, then they will value the Supper highly and receive it frequently. They will welcome their Lord's gracious invitation, "Come unto me, all ye who labor." And they will long for the Sacrament.

FOR REFLECTION

1. Recall or share a time, if possible, when Holy Communion was particularly meaningful to you. Why was the occasion so meaningful? In what ways to you receive comfort and strength from eating and drinking the body and blood of our Lord?

2. The article states, "Sadly, wills often lead to heated arguments. Our Lord's will and testament hasn't fared any better." Explain.

3. Read 1 Corinthians 11:23–26. How does Paul emphasize the importance of the Lord's Supper in Christian worship? In what ways do we "proclaim the Lord's death until he comes" by sharing in His holy meal?

4. What benefits does Christ give to believers in the Lord's Supper? How are the "vertical" and "horizontal" dimensions present in the celebration?

5. What does the Lord's Supper mean for daily living? for the life and mission of your congregation? How does forgiveness, received in the Sacrament, grant us every spiritual blessing?

FOR FURTHER READING

- John 6:1–59
- 1 Corinthians 10:1–31
- Luther's *Small Catechism,* The Sacrament of the Altar

CONFESSION AND ABSOLUTION/REPENTANCE (ARTICLES 11 AND 12)

John T. Pless

> More and more, broken sinners are finding God's peace and healing through private confession and absolution.

Have you ever gone to your pastor for private confession and absolution?

"Isn't that Roman Catholic?" some might answer. "Didn't Luther and the Reformation do away with all that?"

There are other responses, too. The claim that "I can confess my sin directly to God" is used as justification for neglecting private confession. Or, the old Adam might claim that it is the height of arrogance for a pastor to say "I forgive you your sins," because "only God can forgive sins."

The Lutheran Confessions, which set forth the teaching of Holy Scripture and explain what Lutherans believe, say otherwise.

"It is taught among us," says the Augsburg Confession, for example, "that private absolution should be retained and not allowed to fall into disuse" (AC 11).

Martin Luther was no less adamant in the *Large Catechism:* "If you are a Christian, you should be glad to run more than a hundred miles for confession, not under compulsion but rather coming and compelling us to offer it. . . . Therefore, when I urge you to go to confession, I am simply urging you to be a Christian" (LC: "A Brief Exhortation to Confession").

Current wisdom says that people need affirmation, not absolution. David Wells, a prominent observer of contemporary church life, laments that churches have exchanged Biblical reality for "therapeutic models" that "tend to shy away from the concept of sin, or at least to tame it by calling it sickness instead."[1]

Yet the Lutheran Confessions keep us from falling prey to a culture that denies the reality of sin, the need for repentance and the gift of forgiveness. Our Confessions will not let us forget that psychological therapy, for example, as helpful as it sometimes is, can never be a substitute for the Gospel. We are called back to the basics of sin and grace, repentance and faith, confession and absolution.

---

[1]David Wells, *God in the Wastelands: The Reality of Truth in a World of Fading Dreams,* p. 81.

The Repentant Life

The Reformation can be characterized as a struggle over the doctrine of repentance. Luther recognized this early on. In the first of the Ninety-Five Theses, he writes, "When our Lord and Master Jesus Christ said 'Repent' (Matt. 4:17), he willed the entire life of believers to be one of repentance."[2]

Luther was reacting against Rome's doctrine of repentance as an occasional activity in which Christians were required to participate from time to time. He taught that repentance was the natural rhythm of the Christian's life as the Christian daily returns to baptismal death and resurrection.

Repentance is more than "feeling sorry for your sins." According to the Augsburg Confession, "[T]rue repentance is nothing else than to have contrition and sorrow or terror, on account of sin, and yet at the same time to believe the Gospel or absolution (namely, that sin has been forgiven and grace has been obtained through Christ)."

It continues, "and this faith will comfort the heart and again set it at rest. Amendment of life and the forsaking of sin should then follow, for these must be the fruits of repentance, as John says, 'Bear fruit that befits repentance' (Matt. 3:8)" (AC 12).

With a perverted understanding of repentance, it is no wonder that Rome had also twisted private confession, making it a tool of terror rather than a gracious gift of the Gospel.

In the medieval Roman church, private confession was made a requirement of the faithful. Meeting in 1215, the Fourth Lateran Council legislated that "every believer of either gender, after he has arrived at the age of discretion, should himself confess all his sins faithfully at least once a year to his own priest."

As a young monk, Luther faithfully followed the Council's directive. He confessed his sins to his father confessor. But Luther was troubled with uncertainty. Had he sincerely confessed? Had he confessed all of his sins? He was left without the comfort and consolation of the forgiveness of sins.

The Gift of Forgiveness

As he came to know the Gospel, Luther saw Rome's use of private confession as a "slaughter of souls." The sheer gift of the forgiveness of sins in absolution had been replaced by an oppressive demand that sins be enumerated in detail. Confession was made a matter of law, not Gospel.

Confession exists for the sake of the absolution, the pronouncement of forgiveness. Thus, Luther writes in the *Large Catechism,* "We urge you,

[2]*Luther's Works,* American Edition, 31:25.

however, to confess and express your needs, not for the purpose of performing a work but to hear what God wishes to say to you. The Word or absolution, I say, is what you should concentrate on, magnifying and cherishing it as a great and wonderful treasure to be accepted with all praise and gratitude."

Private confession does not consist in enumerating all the sins one has committed. Psalm 19:12, "Who can discern his errors?," is quoted by the Augsburg Confession to demonstrate that recalling and naming all sins would be impossible. Neither do we come to private confession to wallow in self-pity, complain about our sins, or "to get something off my chest."

Rather, we come to confession that we might lay our sins before God and "receive absolution, that is, forgiveness, from the pastor as from God Himself, not doubting, but firmly believing that by it our sins are forgiven before God in heaven" (SC 5).

The Augsburg Confession (Article 12) rejoices in the absolution. All that diminishes absolution is rejected—perfectionists who claim that real Christians cannot fall into sin; the Novatians, who denied absolution to those who sin after Baptism; and the Roman opinion that forgiveness is obtained by human satisfaction rather than through faith.

Absolution is nothing less than the very voice of God Himself. Article 25 expands Article 12: "We also teach that God requires us to believe this absolution as much as if we heard God's voice from heaven, that we should joyfully comfort ourselves with absolution, and that we should know that through such faith we obtain forgiveness of sins."

Spoken from the human lips of a pastor, the absolution is the very Word of the Lord Himself. We see this from Jesus' words to His disciples in Luke 10:16: "He who hears you hears me, and he who rejects you rejects me, and he who rejects me rejects him who sent me."

On Easter evening, the Risen Lord breathes on His apostles, saying to them, "If you forgive the sins of any, they are forgiven; if you retain the sins of any, they are retained" (John 20:21).

God puts His words on the lips of His pastors. And by these words, whether in private confession or after the general confession during the Divine Service, He bestows the forgiveness of sins won for the world by the Lamb of God in His suffering and death. More than mere "assurance," absolution is "the true voice of the Gospel" (Ap 12).

There are signs that private confession is being restored to its rightful place as the ordinary means of pastoral care in many of our congregations. The *Lutheran Worship* hymnal includes an order for "Individual Confession and Absolution" (pp. 310–311). The 1991 edition of *Luther's Small Catechism with Explanation* includes Luther's "A Short Form of Confession."

The goal of recovering the practice of private confession is that Christ Jesus receive all the glory due Him as our only Savior and that we poor sinners receive the full consolation of the forgiveness of sins.

"For we also keep confession, especially because of the absolution, which is the Word of God that the power of the keys proclaims to individuals by divine authority. It would therefore be wicked to remove private absolution from the church. And those who despise private absolution understand neither the forgiveness of sins nor the power of the keys" (Ap 12).

Confession and absolution extol the potency of God's Word and the blood of His Son over our sin.

For Reflection

1. Why is private confession rare in our day? Why might people be reluctant to confess their sins to pastors?

2. What are the "benefits" of private confession with your pastor? When might a Christian seek private confession and absolution?

3. Read Psalm 51:1–12. How do David's words reflect the "rhythm" of Confession and Absolution? In what ways is his psalm a model for Christians today?

4. Why is it important in worship to begin with Confession and Absolution? How does Confession and Absolution "set the tone" for the worship service?

5. The Lord Jesus, like John the Baptizer, began His public ministry with the words, "Repent, for the kingdom of heaven is near" (Matthew 4:17; see also 3:2). What does daily repentance mean in your life?

FOR FURTHER READING

- Matthew 18:1–20
- Galatians 6:1–10
- Luther's *Small Catechism,* Confession and Absolution

How to Use the Sacraments (Article 13)

Charles P. Arand

In the sacraments, God gives and we receive.

This changes everything!

Something like that must have gone through the minds of many 16th century churchmen and theologians as they considered what recovery of the doctrine of justification through faith would mean for the entire life of the church.

Most immediately, the church's message would once again center on the gift and work of Christ, providing believers with the certainty of God's acceptance. But that was only the beginning.

In fact, rediscovering that God declares us "not guilty" of our sins for Christ's sake, through faith, would prove no less revolutionary for theology than adopting the Copernican view of the solar system was for science. The shift from an earth-centered to a sun-centered view led astronomers to rethink the earth's relation to the sun and the planets, and, in turn, the solar system's relation to the stars. In theology, the doctrine of faith would prompt a new look at of every article of Christian doctrine in light of the Gospel.

For example, when the doctrine of the Trinity is considered in this light, it is not viewed in terms of abstract speculation, but in terms of three persons, who, being one God, have given entirely of themselves for our life and salvation. The office of the ministry could no longer be considered an office that makes sacrifices or hands down judgments, but an office that distributes the gifts of Christ's work. Similarly, the church was redefined as those who are bound together by the reception of Christ's gifts.

The doctrine of faith would also change the way the sacraments are handled and the way people make use of them.

The basic statement on proper use of the sacraments is in Article 13 of the Augsburg Confession. This article immediately follows brief statements that describe the distinctive features of Baptism, the Lord's Supper and Absolution. It states:

"It is taught among us that the sacraments were instituted not only to be signs by which people might be identified outwardly as Christians, but that they are signs and testimonies of God's will toward us for the purpose of awakening and strengthening our faith. For this reason they require faith, and they are rightly used when they are received in faith and for the purpose of strengthening faith."

Note the two parts here. First, the sacraments, each in its own way, are signs and testimonies of God's will toward us. By giving Himself and all that He has to us in the sacraments, God makes known His will for us in order that He might arouse and energize faith. Second, they are used properly when they are used in accord with their purpose—that is, when we receive them through faith for the purpose of strengthening our confidence in His care.

Let's see how this works out with reference to God's various means of grace.

Baptism and the Awakening of Faith

The *Small Catechism* describes the work of Baptism this way: Baptism "works the forgiveness of sins, rescues from death and the devil, and gives eternal salvation to all who believe this, as the words and promises of God declare."

Here again we find the two parts of giving and receiving: the gift given in the water; and faith to receive the gift. "How can water do such great things?" Each of us learned to confess, "Certainly not just water, but the word of God in and with the water does these things, along with the faith which trusts this word of God in the water."

And yet our use of Baptism does not stop with the initial reception of Christ's blessings. From Baptism's gifts, we continue to receive strength and power for daily living. In fact, whenever Paul mentions Baptism in his letters, he usually does so within the context of exhorting his readers to live as those who have been born anew, and not as those who still live according to the old life of the flesh (e.g., Romans 6; 1 Corinthians 12; Titus 3).

So it's not surprising that the catechism teaches us to make use of our Baptism each day by dying to sin and rising to new life. To live anew is to live in the daily anticipation and expectation of receiving the goodness of God that endures forever.

Absolution

The rhythm of giving and receiving, dying and rising, that began with Baptism continues in confession and absolution. Although not often thought of as a sacrament today, confession and absolution remains a vital and much-needed means of grace for us.

Once again, the teaching of salvation through faith reshaped the way confession and absolution were used. No longer did people have to wonder whether they remembered each and every sin before it could be forgiven. No longer did they have to wonder whether they felt sorry for sins because they hurt God or because they feared His punishment. No longer did they have to wonder whether or not they had made sufficient recompense to avoid purgatory. Those who came to confession now came in faith—that is, they came eagerly expecting that they would receive the forgiveness of sins.

The *Small Catechism* provides a helpful example in its suggested order for private confession (that also applies to absolution in the Divine Service). The penitent comes to the pastor expressly to seek the forgiveness of sins. Such a one says: "Dear confessor, I ask you please to hear my confession *and to pronounce forgiveness in order to fulfill God's will.*" Following the confession of sins, in which the Christian surrenders all of his or her sins to God, the pastor states, "God be merciful to you and strengthen your faith. Amen." He then proceeds, "Let it be done for you as you believe. And I, by the command of our Lord Jesus Christ, forgive you your sins in the name of the Father and of the Son and of the Holy Spirit. Amen. Go in peace."

Absolution is pronounced; faith hears it and rejoices in it.

The Lord's Supper and the Strengthening of Faith

The pattern of giving and receiving continues, but in a different and unique way. In the Lord's Supper, Christ gives us the forgiveness of sins in His body and blood.

Here we have pure Gospel! What should we do when offered such a gift? Take it! How? By eating and drinking, by believing and trusting.

Consider again how the *Small Catechism* counsels us to receive the body and blood of our Savior in the sacrament of the Lord's Supper. First it asks, "What does 'worthy' mean?" Then, the answer is given, "That person is truly worthy and well-prepared *who has faith in these words:* Given and shed for you for the forgiveness of sins." And as often as we receive this gift with our hearts and mouths, so often it continues to strengthen our faith in that very gift by uniting us with Christ.

The Scriptures, together with the Confessions of our church, identify yet one more function and use of the Lord's supper. In our use and reception of the Lord's body and blood, we publicly confess our faith before the world and announce the blessings of Christ, as Paul says (1 Cor. 11:26): "As often as you do this, you proclaim the Lord's death."

Where the Lord's Supper is celebrated, there the church confesses and proclaims the death of Christ. As such, it marks the existence of the holy Christian church and the place where the baptized gather together.

So on Reformation Day, we not only celebrate the truth that we receive salvation as a free gift from God on account of Christ, but that God bestows it upon us in the sacraments—which we receive through faith, that we might become more confident of His care.

FOR REFLECTION

1. In what ways does God's use of means—Word and sacrament—reveal His love for His fallen children?

2. What are God's promises in Baptism? Why is it God's will that Christian churches baptize infants, children and adults?

3. In what ways is Absolution a sacrament? How is it comforting to hear the pastor's words—as he speaks for Christ—"I forgive you all your sins in the name of the Father and of the Son and of the Holy Spirit"?

4. How do Christians receive the Lord's body and blood "worthily"?

5. How does God mold and shape the Christian life through the means of grace?

FOR FURTHER READING

- 1 Peter 1:3–25
- Luther's *Small Catechism,* Holy Baptism, Confession and Absolution, The Sacrament of the Altar

THE MINISTRY (ARTICLE 14)

Samuel H. Nafzger

The ministry is a gift to the Church from God Himself.

It is only 23 words long—the 14th article of the Augsburg Confession—and 16 have only one syllable: "It is taught among us that nobody should publicly teach or preach or administer the sacraments in the church without a regular call."

But no other topic than the one addressed in this short sentence has been more discussed and debated by Lutherans—or by other Christian churches, for that matter—during the 465 years since the Augsburg Confession was read before the Holy Roman Emperor. Perhaps this is because the doctrine of the ministry has such direct implications for every Christian congregation and, indeed, for every Christian.

The topic of "the ministry" involves not only theology, but also organization, structure and procedures. It involves authority, leadership and personalities. Discussion, even controversy, about "the ministry" so often originates in disputes about power, control and status.

Actually, Article 14 is not the only place where the Augsburg Confession addresses the doctrine of the ministry. Article 5 is titled "The Office of the Ministry," and Article 28 takes up "The Power of Bishops." So, we will need to keep these articles in view, too.

Grounded in the Word

The most striking characteristic of the Augsburg Confession's discussion of "the ministry" is the way the confessors constantly emphasize this doctrine's connection to the *Word.*

Article 4 clearly states that it is God who has instituted "the office of the ministry, that is, provided the Gospel and the sacraments." God has instituted the ministry to make available the means through which we sinful human beings "receive forgiveness of sins and become righteous before God by grace, for Christ's sake, through faith" (AC 4). "The external word of the Gospel" is the only means through which God "gives the Holy Spirit, who works faith, when and where he pleases" (AC 5). The principle here is that "Faith comes from what is heard, and what is heard comes by the preaching of Christ" (Rom. 10:17).

Not only is the *purpose* of the ministry connected to the Word, but in Articles 14 and 28, we see that the Word alone determines the distinction between what we can say about the ministry according to "divine right" and what the church has instituted by "human right."

The Lutherans told the Roman Catholics that it was their "deep desire to maintain the church polity and various ranks of ecclesiastical hierarchy" (Ap 14, 1). But they expressly note that these were "created by human authority." So, when Catholic bishops forced Lutheran pastors "to forsake and condemn the sort of doctrine we have confessed," such bishops could not be acknowledged. The church is present among those "who rightly teach the Word of God and rightly administer the sacraments." It is "not present among those who seek to destroy the Word of God with their edicts"—not even if they are bishops. Faithfulness to the Word makes the difference.

We see this same principle in Article 28, which deals with the power of bishops: "Our teachers assert that according to the Gospel the power of the keys or the power of bishops is a power and command of God to preach the Gospel, to forgive and retain sin, and to administer and distribute the sacraments."

The only power that bishops have by "divine right" is the power "to preach the Gospel, forgive sins, judge doctrine and condemn doctrine that is contrary to the Gospel and exclude from the Christian community the ungodly whose wicked conduct is manifest." In these areas, "parish ministers and churches are bound to be obedient to the bishops according to the saying of Christ in Luke 10:16, 'He who hears you hears me.'"

But any other power has been given to bishops "by virtue of human right." Obedience to all such human ordinances and degrees is proper only "if [the bishops] did not insist on the observances of regulations which cannot be kept without sin." Where this is not the case, "we are bound to follow the apostolic rule which commands us to obey God rather than man."

The ministry, both its purpose and its authority, is grounded in and normed by the Word.

Given to the Church

The fact that the ministry has its foundation in the Word points to a second major truth: the ministry is given to the church. The "power of keys or of bishops *is used and exercised* only by teaching and preaching the Word of God and by administering the sacraments," says the Augsburg Confession. This power is *used* by the bishops; it does not *belong* to them.

Article 5 makes this clear: "To obtain such faith God instituted the office of the ministry, *that is, provided the Gospel and the sacraments.*" The ministry itself is not a means of grace.

Martin Luther, in 1523, seven years before the Augsburg Confession, had written to the Christians in Prague: "Here we take our stand: There is no other Word of God than that which is given all Christians to proclaim. There is no other baptism than the one which any Christian can bestow. There is no other remembrance of the Lord's Supper than that which every Christian can observe and which Christ has instituted. There is no other kind of sin than that which any Christian can bind or loose. There is no other sacrifice than of the body of every Christian. No one but a Christian can pray. No one but a Christian may judge of doctrine. These make the priestly and royal office."[1]

The Lutheran confessors held that these words of Jesus were not directed to Peter alone, nor even only to the apostles: "You are Peter, and on this rock I will build my church, and the powers of death shall not prevail against it. I will give you the keys of the kingdom, and whatever you bind on earth shall be bound in heaven, and whatever you loose on earth shall be loosed in heaven" (Matt. 16:18–19). As the *Treatise on the Power and Primacy of the Pope,* part of our Confessions, puts it, "the church is above the ministers" (Tr 1). And the church is the body of all baptized Christians.

Here we come face to face with the Great Reformer's rediscovery of the precious Scriptural doctrine of the priesthood of all believers. To prove that "wherever the church exists, the right to administer the Gospel also exists," the *Treatise* quotes 1 Peter 2:9: "'You are a royal priesthood.'. . . These words apply to the true church. . . ." As Dr. C.F.W. Walther, a leading 19th century U.S. Lutheran theologian (and first president of The Lutheran Church—Missouri Synod), repeatedly emphasizes, "the pastors use the keys, the congregation possesses them."[2]

Another Lutheran theologian, Francis Pieper, makes the same point: "Since the Christians are the Church, it is self-evident that they alone *originally* possess the spiritual gifts and rights which Christ has gained for, and given to, His Church. Thus St. Paul reminds all believers: 'All things are yours,' 1 Cor. 3:21,22, and Christ Himself commits to all believers the keys of the kingdom of heaven, Matt. 16:13–19; 18:17–20; John 20:22,23, and commissions all believers to preach the Gospel and to administer the Sacraments, Matt. 28:19,20; 1 Cor. 11:23–25. Accordingly, we reject all doctrines by which this spiritual power or any part thereof is adjudged as originally vested in certain individuals or bodies, such as the Pope, or the bishops, or the order of the ministry. . . . The officers of the Church publicly administer their offices only by virtue of delegated powers, conferred on them by the original possessors of such powers, and such administration remains under the supervision of the latter, Col. 4:17. Naturally all Christians have also the right and the duty to judge and decide matters of doctrine, not according to their own notions, of course, but according to the Word of God, 1 John 4:1; 1 Pet. 4:11."[3]

[1]*Luther's Works,* American Edition, Vol. 40, pp. 34–35.
[2]C.F.W. Walther, *The Congregation's Right to Choose Its Pastor,* p. 46.
[3]*Brief Statement of the Doctrinal Position of The Lutheran Church—Missouri Synod,* "The Original and True Possessors of All Christian Rights and Privileges."

Walther emphasized that "the holy ministry or pastoral office is an office distinct from the priesthood of all believers." But he also noted that "it indicates great ignorance if at present many, wherever they find the word 'ministry,' always understand the pastoral office by it. An examination of the old dogmaticians shows what a bad misunderstanding that is."[4]

The Holy Ministry

This brings us to the specific aspect of the ministry taken up in the 14th article of the Augsburg Confession—the doctrine of "the Holy Ministry."

Don't think that anything said thus far in any way detracts from the importance and divine institution of the pastoral office. We have emphasized the ministry in the wide sense only so that what the confessors say about the ministry in the narrow sense might be seen in proper, Scriptural perspective.

Make no mistake. For the Lutheran confessors, the pastoral office—the Scriptures refer to this office by such names as bishop, elder, leader, minister, pastor, shepherd, teacher—is divinely instituted. It exists "by divine right." It is no mere creation of the congregation for reasons of good order and efficiency, although it does serve this purpose.

That a Christian congregation has a shepherd or overseer is God's idea, not some human invention. Paul tells the elders in Ephesus, "Take heed to yourselves and to all the flock, in which the Holy Spirit has made you guardians, to feed the church of the Lord which he obtained with his blood" (Acts 20:28; see Titus 1:5).

Two words in Augsburg 14 need special comment:

First, "publicly." This does not mean out in front of everybody, the opposite of "privately," but rather refers to responsibility and accountability. This understanding of "public" is reflected in a resolution adopted by the Synod in 1992 that reaffirms "the Scriptural position of the church and its ministry as taught in the Lutheran Confessions that God has instituted the office of the pastoral ministry and that the one who holds this office carries it out on behalf of and with accountability to God and those through whom God has called him."

The second is "regular call." The one who holds the office of pastor is not to be a mere volunteer. He is called by God—not directly as were the apostles, but through the congregation—and recognized by the church through the apostolic custom of ordination as a holder of this office:

"The ministry of preaching is conferred by God through the congregation, as holder of all church power, or of the keys, and by its call, as prescribed by God. The ordination of those called, with the laying on of

[4]Walther, p. 136.

hands, is not by divine institution but is an apostolic church ordinance and merely a public, solemn confirmation of the call," says one of 10 theses on ministry written by Walther and approved by The Lutheran Church—Missouri Synod in 1851. (A resolution adopted by the 1995 LCMS convention also observes, "Any man performing the functions of the pastoral ministry as a licensed layman should be called by the congregation which he is serving and ordained into the pastoral office. . . .")

The point in Augsburg 14 is that the office of public ministry is to be exercised not by self-appointed volunteers but by a man whom the congregation has found to possess the Scriptural qualifications for this office: "above reproach, the husband of one wife, temperate, sensible, dignified, hospitable, an apt teacher, no drunkard, not violent but gentle, not quarrelsome, and no lover of money. He must manage his own household well, keeping his children submissive and respectful in every way; for if a man does not know how to manage his own household, how can he care for God's church? He must not be a recent convert, or he may be puffed up with conceit and fall into the condemnation of the devil; moreover he must be well thought of by outsiders, or he may fall into reproach and the snare of the devil" (1 Tim. 3:2–7).

Conflict, or Partnership?

A recent article in the magazine of the Lutheran Church of Australia applies to the United States as well. It says:

"Things *are* changing. The people of God are no longer merely prepared to follow; they want to be involved. They will not glibly swallow what they are taught; they want to learn for themselves. They will not automatically respect the pastor because of who he is; respect has to be earned. People are responding more to shared leadership style rather than a top-down style. Rather than merely supporting the ministry of the pastor, people are looking to undertake their own ministries. . . . These changes can be confusing and unsettling—both for pastors and for the people of God."[5]

How true. In such a context, we can get clear, Scriptural guidance from what the Augsburg Confession says about "the ministry." It rules out pastors seeing ministry as their exclusive domain by "lording it over" their flocks. At the same time, it guards against the false notion that status can be gained for members of the priesthood of all believers by carrying out public ministry in the congregation without a regular call.

Congregations need to recognize the difference between what they want in a pastor, and what the Scriptures say they need. They need to be sensitive to the tension that exists between who their pastor is as a fellow sinner and what he wants to be as one of God's redeemed.

[5]Lutheran Church of Australia, *The Lutheran*, December 1994, p. 404.

Pastors need to be reminded of the privilege that is theirs to serve as an undershepherd of the Good Shepherd, and congregations must not forget that pastors will have to give an account to God for their ministry.

When this happens, conflict can be replaced by joyful partnership, beautifully described by Paul in his letter to the Philippians: "I thank my God in all my remembrance of you, always in every prayer of mine for you all, making my prayer with joy, thankful for your partnership in the Gospel from the first day until now" (1:3–6).

And congregations, for their part, will not find it burdensome to give heed to the apostolic injunction: "Obey your leaders and submit to their authority. They keep watch over you as men who must give an account. Obey them so that their work will be a joy, not a burden, for that would be no advantage to you" (Heb. 13:17).

FOR REFLECTION

1. How are expectations of pastors changing in our world? What are some of the points of conflict between pastors and congregations today?

2. If all believers hold the Keys to the Kingdom, why do only pastors preach, absolve and administer the sacraments in the church?

3. Read 1 Peter 5:1–4. What does the title "shepherd" (pastor) reveal about the duties and responsibilities of those who hold the Office of the Holy Ministry?

4. What does it mean for pastor and people to enjoy a partnership in the Gospel? (See also Philippians 1:3–6.)

5. How can you and your congregation honor and support your pastor(s) in the Ministry of Word and Sacrament?

For Further Reading

- John 21:1–25
- Hebrews 13:1–21
- Luther's *Small Catechism,* Fourth Commandment

A Place for Tradition (Article 15)

Joel Lehenbauer

Are traditions in the church good or bad? Well, it all depends.

Tradition, scoffed British-born poet W.H. Auden, "is the democracy of the dead"—it means letting our ancestors decide what we should do and how we should live. G. K. Chesterton, another Christian poet and novelist, viewed tradition more positively: "Tradition does not mean that the living are dead but that the dead are living."

Whether in politics or in the family or in the church, few issues arouse such passion, debate and even division as the role and value of tradition. The quip is made only *half* in jest that a doctrinal error on Sunday morning is more likely to go unnoticed than an unexpected departure from traditional practice—such as changing the time of the offering or the position of the candelabra.

A 'Middle Way'

The problem of what to do about traditions is not a new one. (One might even say that the church has a tradition of arguing about traditions!) The Lutheran confessors, writing in 1520, admitted in the Apology of the Augsburg Confession: "This subject of traditions involves many difficult and controversial questions. When they are required as necessary, they bring exquisite torture to a conscience that has omitted some observance. On the other hand, their abrogation [elimination] involves its own difficulties and problems" (Ap 15, 49).

Faced with these two equally troubling extremes (requiring or rashly eliminating longstanding traditions), the fathers of Lutheranism proposed a "middle way." To the question, "Are traditions good or bad?," the confessors responded: It all depends.

Traditions are good, they said in the Augsburg Confession, when they "may be observed without sin" and when they "contribute to peace and good order in the church." Traditions are bad when they contradict the Gospel or compromise the authority of God's Word *alone* as divine guide for faith and life (see AC 15).

In a society increasingly marked by frantic schedules and fragmented families, many psychologists, educators and religious leaders today are emphasizing the important role that traditions can play in filling the human need for order, continuity and a sense of "belonging." Books on creating and nurturing "family traditions" convey a message that is ringing true and filling a void for many. Says one book *(Why Not Celebrate!,* by Sara Wenger Shenk), for example:

"Family traditions, when deliberately cultivated, build a sense of identity that will hold a family together from year to year and generation to generation. Celebrative rituals become the vehicle for passing on beliefs and values. Rituals also provide structure in the life of a family. Admittedly, structures can be restrictive; rituals can fall into dead formality. Frameworks that no longer serve a vital purpose must be dismantled. But the solution to meaningless structure need not be a regression to chaos. Bringing order out of disorder or design out of chaos is the creative task of the artist, the Christian. . . ."[1]

In the beginning, God Himself brought "order out of disorder." As those created in His image, we too have a desire—indeed, a need—for "order" and "structure" in our lives (including our spiritual lives).

In the Old Testament era, festivals such as the Passover were instituted by God to serve as regular and repeated reminders of God's saving love and power: "Obey these instructions as a lasting ordinance for you and your descendants. . . . And when your children ask you, 'What does this ceremony mean to you?' then tell them, 'It is the Passover sacrifice to the Lord, who passed over the houses of the Israelites in Egypt and spared our homes when he struck down the Egyptians'" (Ex. 12:24–27).

The New Testament points to such Old Testament ceremonies as "a shadow of the things that were to come; the reality, however, is found in Christ" (Col. 2:17). "Therefore," says Paul, "do not let anyone judge you by what you eat or drink, or with regard to a religious festival, a New Moon celebration or a Sabbath day" (Col. 2:16). Still, Christ's church is reminded that "everything should be done in a fitting and orderly way" (1 Cor. 14:40), since "God is not a God of disorder but of peace" (1 Cor. 14:33).

The first Christians (mostly converts from Judaism) clung to many of the traditions of synagogue worship, though in "Christianized" form. As the church grew and spread, many different traditions, church festivals and forms of worship were developed in order to provide a structured framework for proclaiming, teaching and sharing the Good News of Jesus Christ.

Over the centuries, some of these traditions and forms of worship came to be regarded as more "sacred" and important than God's Word itself. Other traditions contained elements that by their very nature were contrary to the precious, comforting Gospel of salvation through faith alone in Christ alone. When Luther and the reformers spoke out against such errors, they were accused by some of attacking "tradition" as such—of advocating an approach to church life and worship that would ultimately result in chaos.

The Lutheran reformers rejected this accusation as false and ground-

---

[1]Sara Wenger Shenk, *Why Not Celebrate!* (Intercourse, Pa.: Good Books, 1987).

less. Said the confessors, in the Apology: "We gladly keep the old traditions set up in the church because they are useful and promote tranquility" (Ap 15, 38; 220). The church fathers, they said, "observed these human rites because they were profitable for good order, because they gave people a set time to assemble, because they provided an example of how all things could be done decently and in order in the churches, and finally because they helped instruct the common folk. . . . This good order is very becoming in the church and is therefore necessary" (Ap 15, 20–21; 218).

But, said the confessors, something else is also necessary. It is necessary to make it clear that adherence to human traditions is *not* necessary for salvation, nor is it necessary for true unity in the church.

Pharisaical Tendencies

As valuable as traditions are, they can also become harmful and dangerous. When our Lord challenged the traditions of His day regarding the proper observance of the Sabbath, the Pharisees became so enraged that they immediately "went out and plotted how they might kill Jesus" (Mark 12:14). Later, the Pharisees rebuked Jesus for not requiring his disciples to perform the traditional "ceremonial washings."

"You hypocrites!" Jesus responded. "You have let go of the commands of God in order to observe your own traditions!" (Mark 7:8). Worst of all, the Pharisees "shut the kingdom of heaven in men's faces" (Matt. 23:13) by requiring the strict observance of their traditions as necessary for salvation. No wonder Jesus called them "blind guides" and "blind fools" (Matt. 23:16–17).

The Lutheran confessors reacted just as strongly against Pharisaical tendencies in their day to elevate human tradition to the level of divine command and to exalt certain human rites as necessary for salvation. Said our Lutheran forefathers, again in the Apology: "Scripture calls traditions 'doctrines of demons' (1 Tim. 4:1) when someone teaches that religious rites are helpful in gaining grace and the forgiveness of sins. This obscures the Gospel, the blessing of Christ, and righteousness of faith" (Ap 15, 4).

Not only are human traditions not necessary for salvation, said the confessors, they are not even necessary for true unity in the church. "For the true unity of the church it is enough to agree concerning the teaching of the Gospel and the administration of the sacraments. It is not necessary that human traditions or rites and ceremonies, instituted by men, should be alike everywhere," says the Augsburg Confession (AC 7). And its Apology adds, "We believe that the true unity of the church is not harmed by differences in rites instituted by men, although we like it when universal rites are observed for the sake of tranquility" (Ap 7/8, 33).

The Lutheran Confessions use the Latin term *"adiaphora"* to describe those things—like humanly-instituted forms of worship—that are neither *commanded* nor *forbidden* by God in His Word. In these areas, they insist, Christians and Christian congregations are free to decide for themselves what is most helpful and beneficial for carrying out their God-given tasks in their particular locality, as long as God's Word is not compromised and Christian love is exercised (especially concern for the weak in faith—see Romans 14).

"We further believe, teach and confess that the community of God in every place and at every time has the right, authority, and power to change, to reduce, or to increase ceremonies according to its circumstances, as long as it does so without frivolity and offense but in an orderly and appropriate way, as at any time may seem to be most profitable, beneficial, and salutary for good order," says the Formula of Concord (FC SD 10, 9).

The purpose of such rites and ceremonies is not to earn favor with God or to burden consciences with legalistic "rules," but simply "to teach the people what they need to know about Christ" (AC 24, 3). This practical, pastoral concern lies behind all that the Lutheran Confessions have to say about human traditions. If traditions obscure Christ and His saving Gospel, then they must be eliminated or reformed. If traditions serve Christ and edify His church, then they should be honored and preserved—and accompanied by clear, Gospel-centered instruction.

True Unity and Freedom

These truths, of course, must be applied anew in every day and age, as the church re-examines the purpose and usefulness of its traditions. And this is never an easy or noncontroversial task.

In the 1930s, Lutheran theologian Theodore Graebner wrote a book called *The Borderland of Right and Wrong*. In it, he wrestled with the issue of Christian liberty and its application to many of the "traditions" of his day (including the always-sensitive issue of uniformity and/or variety in forms of worship).

On the one hand, Graebner said: "Uniformity in externals, while an adiaphoron, is . . . not a matter of slight importance. The Lutheran Church is a liturgical church, and the essence of liturgy is uniformity. . . . Liberty is good, but license is an extreme which hampers the work of the Church. As it is, by the liberties which our congregations take with the official order of service there has been created a state of liturgical anarchy which is contrary to the spirit of the Reformation and the principles of Luther. . . ."[2]

[2]Theodore Graebner, *The Borderland of Right and Wrong* (St. Louis: Concordia Publishing House, 1951), p. 2.

With equal passion and conviction, however, Graebner goes on to say: "If we have grasped the intention of our Confessions aright, we understand that the Lutheran principle guarantees liturgical freedom in all matters that do not involve a departure from the saving doctrine. By characterizing all forms of worship—this includes architecture, art, garb, and liturgical acts—as indifferent, it condemns those who wish to force upon us the use of certain forms and condemns also those who raise the question of orthodoxy or fellowship when a congregation determines upon a change in the order of service of liturgical arrangements, whatever that change may be (so long as it is not an endorsement of error)."[3]

Graebner strongly advocates the use of Christian persuasion and exhortation in helping others to see the wisdom of maintaining as much uniformity as possible in liturgical forms. But there are two things, he says, that a Christian *cannot* do, no matter how strongly he or she may feel about the usefulness or propriety of a particular form of worship: "(1) He has no right to create parties and divisions in the church on such grounds as these, and (2) he cannot treat as Christians of an inferior order, as disloyal and dangerous to the church, those who do not agree with him."

"How much grief," sighs Graebner, "would not our congregations have been spared if the principle of Christian liberty had always been preserved in such cases of a difference arising over some outward feature in the service of the church!"[4]

Luther once wrote: "It is not a small thing to prohibit where God does not prohibit; to destroy that Christian liberty for which Christ paid His blood; to burden the conscience with sin where there is no sin. . . . Let us confess Christian liberty and not permit the devil to make a law or prohibition and declare things sinful where God has not done so."

"Love is the empress in the domain of ceremonies," added Luther. "Love must decide whether this or that form of worship is to be used. But love is not to decide what we shall believe, what articles of faith we shall hold."

[3]Graebner, p. 4.
[4]Graebner, p. 8.

FOR REFLECTION

1. In what ways is tradition a blessing in the church? How might tradition become a burden—or worse, an obstacle—in the church?

2. What, from the Augsburg Confession, are some "ordinances and traditions instituted by men"? In what ways today do Christians impose human rules upon fellow Christians?

3. Read Mark 7:1–13. What is Jesus' criticism of the religious leaders? In what ways can human traditions "nullify the word of God"? (See also Colossians 2:8.)

4. What aspects and elements of Christian ministry may be adapted to a particular locality, culture, or generation? What can never be adapted to fit our own needs and circumstances?

5. What do you appreciate most about your church's tradition?

How does tradition help you to cherish the Holy Scriptures?

FOR FURTHER READING

- Romans 14:1–15:4.
- 1 Corinthians 8:1–13.

CHRISTIANS AND GOVERNMENT (ARTICLE 16)

David R. Liefeld

It's not easy to keep church and state in a proper relationship. But it's not impossible, either.

From every conceivable direction, Christians today are bombarded with mixtures of church and state.

When socially conscious church bodies take liberal positions on federal and state legislation, for example, they often call them "Christian" positions. And, the New Christian Right often counters with conservative positions that they, too, call "Christian."

Even more common is a simplistic withdrawal by many churches today into a purely "other-worldly" Christianity, with a wall of total separation between church and state. Many Americans seem to *want* their churches to be socially passive.

Are these our only viable options? Are we stuck with church bodies and coalitions of Christians aligned with political agendas, or must we settle for socially and politically passive Christianity?

The Lutheran Confessions offer yet another option—although it must be admitted that it often has not been implemented. The Lutheran Confessions envision such a careful distinction between Law and Gospel that the church is socially relevant—but without political partisanship.

When the Lutheran Confessions were written, church and state were profoundly mixed. In fact, for about a thousand years of the church's history to the time of the Reformation, the church exercised considerable political clout. And at the time of the Reformation, much of that clout was corrupted.

A New Church-State Relationship

Luther's reformation of the church sowed the seeds of a new relationship between church and state. While it did not require their separation (and in many Lutheran lands, the mixture of church and state continued unabated), it does have ample opportunity for growth in the American experiment of democratic pluralism.

Article 16 of the Augsburg Confession makes clear that civil government is good—contrary to those who had concluded that government was inherently corrupted and evil:

"It is taught among us that all government in the world and all established rule and laws were instituted and ordained by God for the sake of good order, and that Christians may without sin occupy civil offices or serve as princes and judges, render decisions and pass sentence according to imperial and other existing laws, punish evildoers with the sword, engage in just wars, serve as soldiers, buy and sell, take required oaths, possess property, be married, etc." This reflects Biblical teaching that the state is God's servant (Rom. 13:1–7) and should be respected for the good it does (Matt. 22:15–22; Titus 3:1–2; 1 Peter 2:13–17).

In other words, the normal affairs of society are of rightful concern to Christians and should occupy their careful attention. It is not more spiritual or pious to ignore them by withdrawing totally into an other-worldly Christianity. In fact, full involvement with the nitty-gritty of politics by American Christians is helpful public witness to the moral law of the "nature's God" to which the Declaration of Independence makes reference.

By the same token, according to Augsburg 16, it is not of the nature of true spirituality to bind the consciences of believers on social and political decisions, as if the Gospel was given for the reformation of society:

"Actually true perfection consists alone of proper fear of God and real faith in God, for the Gospel does not teach an outward and temporal but an inward and eternal mode of existence and righteousness of the heart. The Gospel does not overthrow civil authority, the state, and marriage but requires that all these be kept as true orders of God and that everyone, each according to his own calling, manifest Christian love and genuine good works in his station of life."

Article 28 of the Augsburg Confession, on the power of bishops, clearly teaches the distinctive difference between the purpose and means of church and state.

"Our teachers assert," says the Confession, "that according to the Gospel the power of keys . . . is a power and command of God to preach the Gospel, to forgive and retain sins, and to administer and distribute the sacraments." And, "This power of keys or bishops is used and exercised only by teaching and preaching the Word of God and by administering the sacraments. . . ."

On the other hand, "Temporal authority is concerned with matters altogether different from the Gospel. Temporal power does not protect the soul, but with the sword and physical penalties it protects body and goods from the power of others." Therefore, "the two authorities, the spiritual and the temporal, are not to be mingled or confused. . . . Hence, it [the spiritual power] should not invade the function of the other, should not set up and depose kings, should not annul temporal laws or undermine obedience to government, should not make or prescribe to the temporal power laws concerning spiritual matters." (See John 18:36, Luke 12:14, 2 Cor. 10:4–5, Phil. 3:20, Col. 1:13–14, where the Church is described as a kingdom with spiritual, not temporal, power.)

"Two Kingdoms"

All of this is what has come to be known as the Lutheran doctrine of the "Two Kingdoms." It means that careful distinction between Law and Gospel requires equally careful distinction between the Christian's proper approach to church and state.

God remains Lord—Lord of the Two Kingdoms, Lord of both church and state. But the church exists to proclaim Christ. True spiritual righteousness is rooted in faith created by the Holy Spirit alone at work through the preaching of the Gospel. The state, on the other hand, exists for the sake of the social order. Civil righteousness is rooted in a morality of which all are capable. Civil righteousness is based on the natural law, which accuses evildoers and rewards those who serve the needs of their neighbors and community (see Rom. 13:3 and 1 Peter 2:14).

For Luther and the Augsburg Confession, the normative principles of the church are faith and love, while the normative principles of the state are reason and justice. Reason may not be appropriate to the righteousness of faith, but it is an essential part of government. Understanding this is critical to a proper understanding of church and state.

Reason and force are integral to government, but dare not be imported into the creation of true spirituality. People should not be forced to believe rightly, although government can and must force people to behave within the bounds of generally accepted morality. Government should not require people to be Christians, just as churches should not require Christians to be Republicans or Democrats, or to adopt politically partisan positions about which sincere Christians might reasonably disagree.

The Gospel does not legislate civil righteousness. It is not more spiritual or more pious to construct a so-called "Christian society." Christians must express their faith in good works, but they can and will disagree about exactly how to do that. So also Christians can work vigorously on political agendas without expecting agreement among their brothers and sisters in the faith. Unfortunately, many churches today have crossed the line to endorse political agendas.

How, then, does the church remain socially relevant without binding the consciences of its members on social issues?

First of all, we need to acknowledge that some social issues, such as abortion, are so clearly addressed in God's Word and (just as importantly) so central to the basic task of government that the church can speak to it with authority. Even here, however, prudence is required in distinguishing the Scriptural concern for the sanctity of life from the political means by which that might be accomplished, about which equally committed Christians might disagree. For, in each and every instance of social concern, the church must discern that speaking which will preserve its unity in the Gospel. This requires prudent sensitivity to the ease with which the church can become politicized.

Nevertheless, the church *can* help its members confront social issues without partisanship. This is best done in dialogue that provides opportunity for give and take between clergy and laity, rather than the strictly one-way communication characteristic of the sermon. Bible classes and congregational forums may be very helpful in this. The laity, with all its diverse gifts, has knowledge and expertise on technical subjects that church-body staff and pastors lack. The church must demonstrate respect for this expertise.

Thus, the church and its clergy should bring to bear the resources of Scripture and the Lutheran Confessional heritage in such a way that social awareness is increased through teaching about sin, the moral law and Christian citizenship. But this must be done with prudent sensitivity to basic political and philosophical differences that exist among Christians as they seek to implement their faith in good works of love. Equivalent, sincere concern for the poor and the oppressed, for instance, may well lead to quite different political convictions among equally committed Christians about how the government should address such an important concern.

Lutherans believe that there is a place for Biblical Law to guide Christians in their struggle to address social and political issues (see 1 Cor. 10:31 and Col. 3:17, where Christians are called to apply their Christian faith to *all* of life). Yet, we dare not confuse the complex and ambiguous task of applying our Christian faith to politics with the clear and ultimately decisive matter of knowing and believing the Gospel (Rom. 1:16 and 3:28).

FOR REFLECTION

1. What are some key issues in church and state relations today?

2. Why is it important to distinguish, in both doctrine and politics, between the two kingdoms—between God's rule in the church and God's rule/authority in the state?

3. Read Romans 13:1–7. Summarize, in your own words, a Christian attitude toward authority and law.

4. How might Christians respond to laws that are contrary to God's word and harmful to the Church?

5. Why must the church and church leaders be careful about their involvement in partisan political issues?

FOR FURTHER READING

• 1 Peter 2:13–25

THE RETURN OF CHRIST (ARTICLE 17)

David P. Scaer

Christians look forward to Christ's return—not with dread, but with confidence.

The 16th-century Lutheran reformers and the Roman Catholics disagreed on many things. But they did not disagree one bit on what the Augsburg Confession said about the return of Christ:

"It is also taught among us that our Lord Jesus Christ will return on the last day for judgment and will raise up all the dead, to give eternal life and everlasting joy to believers and the elect but to condemn ungodly men and the devil to hell and eternal punishment" (AC 17).

Unfortunately, agreement on Christ's visible return to judgment is not so universal today. Many Christians no longer believe in a real or physical return of Jesus, but instead look for His return in the lives of Christians and their efforts to improve society. This thinking was at the heart of the "Social Gospel" movement early in this century and even attracted some church leaders to the promises of socialism—and, in extreme cases, of communism.

But this is not what Scripture means when it speaks of Christ's return.

When the disciples kept staring into space after Christ had ascended out of their view, two angels appeared. "'Men of Galilee,' they said, 'why do you stand here looking into the sky? This same Jesus, who has been taken from you into heaven, will come back in the same way you have seen him go into heaven'" (Acts 1:11).

Jesus Himself spoke of His return and what He would do on that day: "'When the Son of Man comes in his glory, and all the angels with him, he will sit on his throne in heavenly glory. All the nations will be gathered before him, and he will separate the people one from another as a shepherd separates the sheep from the goats'" (Matt. 25:31–32).

Heaven and Hell

So, what happens to the "sheep" and "goats"?

Jesus continues, "'He will put the sheep on his right and the goats on his left. Then the King will say to those on his right, "Come, you who are blessed by my Father; take your inheritance, the kingdom prepared for you since the creation of the world. . . ." Then he will say to those on his left, "Depart from me, you who are cursed, into the eternal fire prepared for the devil and his angels. . . ." Then they will go away to eternal punishment, but the righteous to eternal life'" (Matt. 25:33–34,41,46).

A Gallup poll in 1993 found that 80 percent of Americans believe in a Judgment Day when all people will be called to answer to God for their sins. Nearly the same number believe there is a heaven, and most of those polled think they have a "good" or "excellent" chance of going there.

But only 60 percent of the American adults surveyed said they believe in hell, where the wicked will be punished.

Although the Lutherans and Roman Catholics agreed on the particulars of Christ's return, there were other ideas even back in Reformation days. The "odd men out" were radical reformers called Anabaptists, who denied that unbelievers and Satan were destined to hell.

Denial of hell is a view as old as Origen, an early Greek church father, dating to around A.D. 200. And it's not uncommon today across the religious spectrum, from small sects and large Protestant denominations to Roman Catholics.

Most Americans *say* they believe in hell but are unwilling to say that anyone, especially someone they know, is there. Any thought about a hell for those who reject Christ is foreign to their thinking.

Instead, hell is understood as little more than life's miseries. As real as these miseries are, though, heaven and hell in the Bible—and therefore in Lutheran doctrine—are realities that belong to the afterlife.

Believers in an afterlife often say they think of it in terms of a *better* life. If that's so, though, why do so many fear dying? Perhaps they are not entirely successful in ridding their minds of a final judgment and a subsequent hell.

As uncomfortable as the thought of hell is, what we believe about it is associated with what we believe about God and Christ's atonement. A hell in which evildoers are punished is the ultimate statement of a *moral* God. Without the threat of punishment, transgression has no meaning. We are more likely to disobey the posted speed limit if enforcement is lax. God's command to Adam and Eve not to eat from the tree of the knowledge of good and evil carried a threat of death. Without threat, law has no meaning.

The seriousness of Christ's death can be understood only when we believe in a God who punishes Him for our sin. The Nicene Creed says that Christ *"for us men and for our salvation* came down from heaven" and that He *"suffered* and was buried." On the cross, Jesus cried out, "My God, my God, why have you forsaken me?" (Matt. 27:46). Christ knew hell by being forsaken by God in our place. This points to the enormity of our transgression. But it also provides us a firm hope at the judgment.

The Resurrection of the Dead

The Roman Catholics completely agreed with the Lutherans "that at the consummation of the world Christ will appear and raise all the dead, granting eternal life and eternal joys to the godly but condemning the ungodly to endless torment with the devil," as the Apology of the Augsburg Confession puts it.

Both still confess this in the Apostles' and Nicene Creeds, but most explicitly in the Athanasian Creed, the creed often used on Trinity Sunday: "At [Christ's] coming all men shall rise again with their bodies and shall give an account of their own works. And they that have done good shall go into life everlasting; and they that have done evil, into everlasting fire."

As harsh as these words sound, they are taken almost verbatim from Jesus: "those who have done good to the resurrection of the life and those who have done evil to the resurrection of judgment" (John 5:29). Good deeds by which Christians are judged are Christ's works of mercy done to others. Yes, we are saved by grace alone through faith alone, but these works show the world—now and at the judgment—that *true faith* is present in us.

From earliest times, the church has understood "the resurrection of the body" as a *physical* resurrection—and even substituted "flesh" for "body" to make this clear.

It seems that during Paul's life, some people twisted his words about the resurrection of a "spiritual body" (1 Cor. 15:44) to mean that only the soul lived on after death and that the body remained in the grave (2 Peter 3:15-16). To get Paul's meaning, put "s" in upper case, so it reads "*Spiritual.*" The body is raised by the Holy *Spirit*. Using "flesh" for "body" left no room for the common idea among ancient peoples that after death, souls were doomed to perpetual, often murky existence, with no resurrection of the *body*.

To be sure, the souls of believers live on after death—but in bliss, in a state of heightened consciousness, and they join the angels in praising God (Ap 21). This intermediate state of blessedness climaxes in the resurrection, when body and soul will be rejoined in ultimate and permanent glorification (1 Thess. 4:13–18). The curse of Gen. 3:19, returning man to dust, will be reversed, and God's first purpose of man as both body and soul (Gen 2:7) will be perfectly realized.

Lutherans questioned the practice of prayers to the saints (AC 21) and masses for the dead (AC 25), but neither they nor the Roman Catholics questioned the soul's survival after death. The conviction that the soul survives death has particular meaning in the face of Buddhism and other popular forms of Eastern thought in which the soul at death loses its separate identity in nirvana.

Millennialism

While all parties during the Reformation agreed on Christ's visible return, the Anabaptists prepared for His return by trying to establish an *earthly* kingdom. The basis of their failed social experiment is a false teaching called "millennialism," a term from the Latin for a thousand years.

Today, many, if not most, fundamentalists and "Evangelicals" are millennialists, believing that Christ will establish an earthly kingdom when He returns. Though not agreed on the details, nearly all millennialists find support in a literal understanding of the picture-language reference to "1,000 years" in Rev. 20:2–7.

Millennialism is popular in many forms, especially among Americans. In the last century, Shakers renounced marriage and lived in communes. The more successful (and decidedly non-Christian) Latter Day Saints, known as Mormons, established their own communities, most notably in Salt Lake City.

A moderating view is common to fundamentalists and Neo-Evangelicals who aim to make America a "Christian" nation in which church and state are to be partners in promoting moral behavior through legislation. Prohibition, for example, was a failed attempt to do this, but its purpose survives in local "blue laws" that still regulate the sale of alcoholic beverages. Today, the energies of these groups are directed toward establishing political-action groups, such as the Christian Coalition, to elect candidates and pass laws to further "Christianize" the nation.

These groups often are also aligned with Zionist Jews in finding a legal basis for the modern state of Israel in God's promise to Abraham and in certain Old Testament prophecies. Millennialists are already advertising celebrations in Israel for the year 2000, a multiple of 1,000.

Millennialists agree in their interpretation of John 5:29 that there will be one resurrection for the saints and another a thousand years later for the damned (but "pre-millennialists" hold that Christ will appear at the first resurrection, and "post-millennialists" at the second one). Some hold that true believers will be "raptured," or swept into heaven, leaving others behind on the earth, where Christ will rule for a thousand years.

These views, diverse as they are, are sufficiently similar to the errors of the Reformation-era Anabaptists to be included in the Augsburg Confession's condemnation of those who "teach that, before the resurrection of the dead, saints and godly men will possess a worldly kingdom and annihilate all the godless."

Also disturbing is how millennialists apply Bible prophecies to world events, especially in Israel. Some desire to rebuild the Jerusalem temple. For Lutherans, any suggestion that the temple can be rebuilt is a denial that *Christ* is God's temple, to which we belong by faith.

Millennialist fascination with Israel is a denial that Christ has fulfilled both the prophecies and the content of the Old Testament. Our disagreement with millennialism is not about the interpretation of this or that Bible passage, but is based on an entirely different approach. *Christ is the content of Holy Scripture, and our Confessions do not allow for the fulfillment of Scripture outside of* Him.

In the Meantime

God doesn't have to wait until the Last Day to exercise His judgment. Luther was aware, for example, of God's judgment coming upon the Germans because they did not accept the Gospel that was restored by the Reformation. We cannot put ourselves in God's place, but we are aware that God passes judgment by withholding the Gospel from people who do not accept it.

Throughout the Bible, God threatens and brings judgment into the present in preparation for the Last Day. The flood that destroyed the world in Noah's day and the exile of the Jewish nation into Babylon were seen by the later prophets and the New Testament as God's judgment against unbelief. Jesus prophesied the destruction of Jerusalem as a punishment for those who did not accept Him. Its destruction in A.D. 70 stands as a sign of the complete world judgment on the Last Day.

These historical crises point to the final judgment when Jesus will appear.

Each celebration of Holy Communion also focuses the congregation on that final judgment and prepares us to meet Jesus as our Judge on the Last Day (1 Cor 11:26). The signers of our Lutheran Confessions made their confession within the reality of the Last Day. They were willing to appear "before the tribunal of our Lord Jesus Christ" with this faith (Preface to the Book Of Concord).

True faith in Jesus Christ gives Christians confidence on that day. As it is written, "Just as man is destined to die once, and after that to face judgment, so Christ was sacrificed once to take away the sins of many people; and he will appear a second time, not to bear sin, but to bring salvation to those who are waiting for him" (Heb. 9:27–28).

FOR REFLECTION

1. How do non-Christians generally respond to the "end of the world"?

2. What are some typical views of hell in today's world? Why do many people reject the notion of God's judgment?

3. Read 1 Thessalonians 4:13–18. How might St. Paul's words have provided comfort to grieving Christians? How does the return of Christ and the hope of resurrection "encourage" Christians today?

4. What is Millennialism? In what ways does Millennialism contradict and threaten the Gospel?

5. How does the promise of Christ's return affect your relationships? your work and priorities? your stewardship?

FOR FURTHER READING

- John 14:1–14
- 1 Corinthians 15:1–58

FREE WILL—OR NOT (ARTICLE 18)

Thomas Manteufel

> We humans can exercise a lot of freedom—whether or not to eat or drink or visit a friend, for example. But we don't have the natural willpower to believe in Jesus Christ.

How is a human being like a stone?

This sounds like a child's riddle. But it has always been a very serious matter for Lutherans.

The Formula of Concord, one of our Lutheran Confessions, claims that in a person's own conversion or regeneration "he can as little begin, effect, or cooperate in anything as a stone." He or she is no more capable of believing in Christ than a stone and has the same freedom of will that a stone has. The Augsburg Confession (AC 18) had made the same point long before.

But what exactly did the Confessions mean? Let us first make sure that we are clear on what they were *not* saying about humankind.

Not Like a Stone

The Lutheran Confessions are not claiming that human beings have no free will at all. The Augsburg Confession describes what they can do by their natural abilities to decide and will, in the natural condition into which they are born: "Man possesses some measure of freedom of the will which enables him to live an outwardly honorable life and to make choices among the things that reason comprehends." Here they are no stones.

By natural reason and will, one can consider his situation and make decisions to organize his life and solve his problems, like Lot choosing his land (Gen. 13:11). The Augsburg Confession, quoting St. Augustine, gives some examples: "whether or not to labor in the fields, whether or not to eat or drink or visit a friend, whether to dress or undress, whether to build a house, take a spouse, engage in a trade."

Man can use his freedom of choice in moral activities — for instance, to keep his hands from theft or adultery, or to murder and worship idols. The attainment of a life that is considered good and right by civil society is often called "civil righteousness." It has great value for social order and is to be encouraged.

The Lutheran Confessions do not agree with the notion that we have no free will, or that our life and behavior are fixed for us by the stars, or environment, or upbringing. People (or their lawyers) have argued that they should not be held guilty for atrocious acts, because of pigeonhole-making factors in their lives. But, human beings do have freedom and responsibility for their actions.

However, the Augsburg Confession adds this qualification: Man has "*some measure* of freedom of will" to do all these things.

In deciding to adopt and pursue a certain course of action, for example, he meets many limitations, factors over which he has no control, tangles he cannot unravel. Above all, without God's blessing and agreement to give success to his attempts, he will not succeed. "In his heart a man plans his course, but the Lord determines his steps" (Prov. 1:9). He is not the master of his life.

As for civil righteousness, it is never even as good or abundant as it could be, because of the powerful corrupt tendencies in the human race.

Still, a certain question always comes up: Since we do have at least some free will to decide not to murder, to take corrective action, and the like, can we use our will for turning toward God and becoming a believer in Christ? Many people have thought so. As Dr. Ewald Plass stated the problem in *The Abiding Word,* "three possibilities exist. Either God alone brings a man to faith, or man works faith within himself, or he is converted by the cooperative effort of God and himself."

The first possibility—that only God can bring someone to faith—states that here a person *is* like a stone, and the Lutheran Confessions insist that this is true.

Like a Stone

Says the Augsburg Confession, "without the grace, help, and activity of the Holy Spirit man is not capable of making himself acceptable to God, of fearing God and believing in God with his whole heart, or of expelling evil lusts from his heart." Human beings simply cannot choose to become Christians and to perform acts that will achieve that lofty goal.

The Confession draws its thought from the Biblical doctrine of "original sin," which says that everyone who is not born again is spiritually blind, dead and hostile to God (2 Cor. 4:4; Eph. 2:1; Rom. 8:7). Because of inherited sinfulness, human nature and will "cannot produce the inward affections, such as fear of God, trust in God," says the Confession.

The Augsburg Confession cites 1 Cor. 2:14: "The man without the Spirit does not accept the things that come from the Spirit of God, for they are foolishness to him, and he cannot understand them, because they are spiritually discerned." So even when the unregenerated person chooses to do the finest deeds of civil righteousness, they are still works done without faith in the Lord. And, "without faith it is impossible to please God" (Hebrews 11:6).

Therefore, no one should speak of being converted by "inviting Christ into my heart" or becoming a Christian by "deciding to come to Christ." The unconverted flesh cannot create its own faith. Martin Luther asked, "How must one begin to become pious, or what must one do to move God to begin to work in us?" He answered, "Whatever you begin is sin and remains sin, no matter how pretty it may appear to us." He added: "Your faith comes from Him, not from you."

But if one has joyfully heard and believed the Good News that Jesus is his Savior, God has already kindled faith in the heart through the Gospel! Will power has nothing to do with it.

By the same token, free will is not the cause of God's election of those who are saved. Before they believed or desired anything, He chose them from the beginning to be saved through belief in the truth (2 Thessalonians 2:13). This issue has caused unfortunate controversies, such as our own church body's long conflict many years ago with the idea that God elected those whom He foresaw would come to faith by the decision of their own free will. A character in a novel of the time put it this way: "One can't expect to be elected unless he agrees to be a candidate." But no one can raise up faith in his own heart; it must originate with God.

Like a Resurrected Body

The Confessions also use the imagery of the grave, as in the Formula of Concord: "As little as a corpse can quicken itself to bodily, earthly life, so little can man who through sin is spiritually dead raise himself to spiritual life." Coming to faith is a *spiritual resurrection* and new creation by God.

The believer is like a person raised from the dead. After this "resurrection," all his decisions, confessions of Christ and prayerful invitations to Him are expressions of the new life as it goes on to "continue in the grace of God" (Acts 13:43).

In this resurrected state, the Christian's will is renewed. It can use its deciding powers in a sanctified way and is free to cooperate with God by making choices about how to serve Him, as did Moses (Hebrews 11:25), Mary (Luke 10:42), and the disciples (Mark 14:7).

We are no longer stones, but new creatures—alive in the power of Jesus Christ.

For Reflection

1. What types of freedom do we daily enjoy in today's world?

Why is freedom so fundamental to our existence and happiness?

2. Why, in your view, do many people think that humans can believe in God by their own free will and choice?

3. Read Ephesians 2:1–10. How does St. Paul picture our existence apart from God's grace? How specifically has God's grace changed our daily life and eternal future?

4. Respond: "Christ saved me in His death and resurrection, but it's up to me to choose to believe in Him."

5. In what ways is believing in Christ for salvation similar to the resurrection from the dead? (See John 5:24–27.) What comfort do you find in the Lord's words, "I am the resurrection and the life"? (John 11:25)

For Further Reading

• Romans 8:1–17

THE ONE MEDIATOR
(ARTICLE 21)

David L. Mahsman

Jesus brings us and God back together. And He's the only One who can.

You no doubt pray to Jesus. But did you know that Jesus prays for *you?*

In the past, Jesus lived, died, rose bodily and ascended. At some future point, He will return in judgment. These truths we have already examined in this little book.

But what about now?

Now, Christ Jesus, the Son of God, sits at the right hand of the Father—picture language meaning that He once again fully exercises His divine power, something He did not do while on earth—and prays for you and me.

Jesus praying for you and me is nothing new. He prayed for us already when He was still on earth and facing certain death. After praying to His Father for the disciples gathered with Him before His arrest, Jesus went on to pray "for those who will believe in me through their [the apostles'] message" (John 17:20).

"Father," Jesus prayed, "I want those you have given me to be with me where I am, and to see my glory, the glory you have given me because you loved me before the creation of the world" (v. 24). He prayed that you and I would reach the final goal of the faith God has given us: eternal life and glory with Christ.

Jesus still prays for us today. "Christ Jesus, who died—more than that, who was raised to life—is at the right hand of God and is also interceding for us," writes St. Paul (Rom. 8:34). And, says the Letter to the Hebrews, "Therefore he is able to save completely those who come to God through him, because he always lives to intercede for them" (Heb. 7:25).

Imagine what powerful prayer—on our behalf—that this is. God praying to God.

We need His prayer, because we are assaulted by evil on all sides.

Evil slaps at us from the outside. We have seen the destruction that can be wreaked upon us by the forces of nature. Meanwhile, other people assault us with violence, for example, or through injustice or evil gossip.

We are assaulted from within, too. Our own sinfulness alienates us from God and from others. We disappoint others, even those closest to us, and they disappoint us. Life can disappoint us, too, and we wonder,

"What's the point?" We become disgusted with our own behavior. We know that God can't be very happy with us. Finally, we see death coming and can't do a thing about it.

Enter the "Middleman"

Enter Jesus. God Himself becomes a man and bridges the gap that we have created between Him and us. He, and He alone, has the power to save us from ourselves and from His Father's wrath.

Jesus is the *middleman* between us and God the Father. That's the basic meaning of "mediator" when Paul writes, "For there is one God and one mediator between God and men, the man Christ Jesus, who gave himself as a ransom for all men . . ." (1 Tim. 2:5-6). As both fully God and fully human, Jesus trades places with us. He takes on our sin, our guilt and our punishment and gives us His perfection, His holiness and His glory.

"When the merciful Father saw that we were being oppressed through the Law, that we were being held under a curse, and that we could not be liberated from it by anything," wrote Martin Luther, "He sent His Son into the world, heaped all the sins of all men upon Him, and said to Him: 'Be Peter the denier; Paul the persecutor, blasphemer, and assaulter; David the adulterer; the sinner who ate the apple in Paradise; the thief on the cross. In short, be the person of all men, the one who has committed the sins of all men. And see to it that you pay and make satisfaction for them.'"

This Jesus did. And this is what stands behind His prayers to the Father for our sake. If we sin, St. John writes, "we have one who speaks to the Father in our defense—Jesus Christ, the Righteous One. He is the atoning sacrifice for our sins, and not only for ours but also for the sins of the whole world" (1 John 2:1b-2).

In his book *Speaking the Gospel Today*, Dr. Robert Kolb talks about Jesus, our Middleman, bridging the gulf between us and God from both sides. As God, He reaches across the gulf to draw us to Himself. As a human being, He makes possible our reunion with the Father.

"Like the shepherd willing to risk all to bring the straying sheep back to the flock (Luke 15:3–7; John 10:14–16), this mediator draws the erring children into the arms of the waiting Father (Luke 15:11–32)," Kolb writes.

"Jesus is the mediator who brings together two lovers who have drifted apart, and for whom life can never be complete until they are again in fellowship," he continues. "The human creature, weak and sinful and helpless, needs God. Jesus is the mediator, the middleman, who stands in the midst, and draws us and God together again. . . ."

Only One Middleman

By the time of the Reformation, people had begun to look to someone other than Christ Jesus as their "middleman." Many were praying to the saints and to the mother of Jesus and asking for *their* intercession with God.

In Article 21 of the Augsburg Confession, the Lutherans dealt with this issue, saying that "it cannot be proved from the Scriptures that we are to invoke saints or seek help from them." And if a teaching, or doctrine, couldn't be proved from Scripture, it had to be rejected.

"'For there is one mediator between God and men, Christ Jesus' (1 Tim. 2:5), who is the only savior, the only high-priest, advocate, and intercessor before God (Rom. 8:34)," they said. "He alone has promised to hear our prayers. Moreover, according to the Scriptures, the highest form of divine service is sincerely to seek and call upon this same Jesus Christ in every time of need. 'If anyone sins, we have an advocate with the Father, Jesus Christ the righteous' (1 John 2:1)."

This is where confessional Lutherans stand yet today. There is only one true God and only one way—through Jesus Christ—for anyone to know Him.

This doesn't sit too well with our culture. Many people today have a hard time with the notion that Jesus provides the only possible access to God the Father.

There's nothing new, of course, about non-Christians feeling this way. After all, the Romans persecuted the early Christians at least in part because of their exclusive claims for Christ. As a result, they wouldn't acknowledge Caesar as a god.

It's not even new for Christians to lose sight of the fact that Christ alone can bring us and God together. We've already taken note of prayers to saints and Mary. And Satan is always trying to convince us that we can approach God at least in part on the basis of our own effort rather than entirely on account of Christ alone.

But what is especially troubling today is that so many people who claim to be Christian question whether Jesus is necessary *at all*.

Survey-researcher George Barna writes that "three out of 10 born-again Christians agree that all good people will go to heaven regardless of the nature of their relationship with Jesus Christ."

"Sadly, the vast majority of Catholics (65 percent) agree with the good-behavior-opens-the-gates philosophy," Barna adds. "A majority of Methodists believed this, too (51 percent). Even one-third of all Lutherans (35 percent) and one-quarter of all Baptists (26 percent) accepted this thinking."

Recently, a Lutheran pastor was invited to speak about our church to a congregation of another church body. The minister at that other church, I'm told, opened the session with this introduction:

"There are many pathways to the Truth . . . many forms of the Truth. . . . We are an inclusive church. We believe the Scriptures contain God's intent, . . . not necessarily His Word. We are not a church with doctrines and creeds. Interpretations can be cultural and apply to the individual. Scripture is not the central focus of our church, but rather we focus on individual feelings. . . ."

Feelings change. To build on feelings is to build on shifting sand.

The Reformers built on rock. They were certain that what they confessed is true, because what they confessed was firmly grounded in God's Word. They believed the words Jesus prayed to His Father, "Your word is truth" (John 17:17). So do we.

And we believe Jesus when he said, "I am the way, the truth and the life. No one comes to the Father except through me" (John 14:6).

That sounds harsh and cruel to many ears. To many, one religion—or no religion—is as good as another. To many, it makes sense to see heaven as the reward for a life of charity and good deeds. To many, it is obnoxious and self-righteous to claim that some will be saved and some will be lost eternally.

But it is the truth. And we must never forget it.

We must never forget it because our own salvation depends on trusting only in the merits of Jesus, and nothing else. What's more, the salvation of so many others depends on Christians acting upon this truth by bringing the Good News of Jesus Christ to their neighbors and friends, and even across cultures throughout their country and world.

It's tremendously good news that God became a man, lived and suffered and died in our place, rose from the dead and gives us eternal life as a free gift. That's Good News to share with everyone. That's the Good News that there *is* a name under heaven by which we are saved (Acts 4:12).

Don't cut out the Middleman. Without Christ Jesus, we would still be separated from God and there would be no hope for us. But because He *is* our Mediator, we need fear no evil of any sort—neither that which attacks us from the outside, nor that which is part and parcel of our own human nature.

Because Jesus Christ is our Mediator, we are God's children and He is our loving Father. And so we have life, and we have it to the full.

This we believe, teach and confess.

FOR REFLECTION

1. What is the role of a mediator in today's world?

In what ways do mediators help in family life? in business?

2. What other types of "mediators" do people often place between themselves and God?

3. Read Hebrews 12:18–24. How does the passage illustrate the difference between judgment and grace, Law and Gospel? What does it mean to have Jesus as "the mediator of a new covenant"?

4. "Jesus prays for you." What does the Savior ask His Father on our behalf? How does this promise give you hope in times of hardship and personal loss?

5. In what ways can you be Christ's messengers of reconciliation to your friends and acquaintances today? (See 2 Corinthians 5:18–21.)

FOR FURTHER READING

• John 17

ANSWERS AND COMMENTS

God and His Creation (Article 1)

1. Some people view God as a liberating Spirit, a non-judgmental Friend, a cosmic presence, etc. Many people are influenced by media, popular literature, New Age books and music, friends, and a variety of other sources. Ironically, the one source of truth, the Holy Scriptures, is often ignored or neglected.

2. God reveals that He is Creator and Redeemer (v. 1), who calls and summons His people by name and protects them through all types of adversity (v. 2). God is Lord, the personal God ("your God"), who is both holy and righteous, and who saves His people from destruction. In Christ, God has revealed Himself as our gracious Savior.

3. The Christian church has always acknowledged God as "creator and preserver of all things." Anything less attributes the splendor of the created universe to human achievement or random forces.

4. God's grace and goodness in Christ extends to every facet of our lives. Luther's explanation includes the gift of our body and soul, our reason and senses, family and friends, property and possessions, daily sustenance, protection from danger and evil, and many other blessings in life.

5. The triune God is always active in our lives, pouring out upon us His rich blessings, above all, the gift of faith in Christ. Through Baptism, the Father, Son and Holy Spirit dwell in our hearts, calling us to daily repentance and trust in the Savior's work of redemption, nurturing our faith through the Gospel and the sacraments.

Sin (Article 2)

1. Some people view sin as a minor violation of God's commandments or, more simply, as the simple mistakes we make in everyday life. To deny or minimize the seriousness of sin is to trivialize the holiness of God as well as the sacrifice of Jesus for the sins of the world.

2. Every sin is, at root, a failure to "fear, love, and trust God above all things", for we either put our needs and reputation first or we seek deliberately to hurt others. In both cases, we demonstrate our lack of respect, our ingratitude, and our stubborn unbelief and rebellion toward our Creator.

3. "No one seeks God" (v. 10): The First and Third commandments. "No one who does good" (v. 12): All commandments. "Their tongues practice deceit" (v. 13): The Eighth Commandment. "Their mouths are full of cursing and bitterness" (v. 14): The Fourth, Ninth and Tenth Commandments. "Their feet are swift to shed blood" (v. 15): The Fifth

Commandment. "No fear of God" (v. 18): The First Commandment. The first and foremost purpose of the law, for fallen humankind, is to show all people their sinfulness: "through the law we become conscious of sin" (v. 20).

4. Christian preaching and teaching must include both Law and Gospel so that all people might recognize their sin, acknowledge their need and their inability to redeem themselves, and look to God's mercy in Christ for forgiveness and life. Christians, too, need to hear the Law, so that they may understand God's will for holy living and daily remember their sin and need for the Savior.

5. Jesus' death and resurrection is our assurance that God has solved our fundamental problem and will continue to guide us and provide His strength—through Word and sacrament—for all of life's opportunities and challenges.

Jesus Christ, "His Only Son, Our Lord" (Article 3)

1. Some common views today are that Jesus is (1) a teacher; (2) a prophet; (3) a guide to spiritual enlightenment; (4) a holy man; or (5) simply a relgious figure from the past. Some views minimize His role as Lord, Savior, or returning Judge of the universe.

2. In order to be the true Savior of the world, Jesus is God, the Son of the Father, eternal, equal in glory, honor, and power. In order to be true substitute for us, Jesus is also fully human. Only then could He know and sympathize with our weakness, and in His death and resurrection redeem and eternally save fallen human beings.

3. For example, Jesus in His humiliation was willing to suffer everything—even death—for our salvation. In His exaltation, Jesus rules the universe and His church as Lord. He guides and protects us by His almighty power, triumphantly displayed in His resurrection from the dead, ascension and return as Judge of the world.

4. Answers will vary depending upon the many titles, but each assures us that Jesus, true God and true Man, has brought us into the kingdom of God through His death and resurrection.

5. Christ's benefits today—as forever—are forgiveness, fellowship, life eternal, salvation, all bestowed and sealed in Word and sacrament. We receive His gifts weekly in worship, daily in reading and meditating upon His Word, and moment to moment as He leads and strengthens us to serve Him.

Justification: What It's All About (Article 4)

1. People may search for meaning and fulfillment in personal, specific ways through financial security, reputation, work success and advancement, pleasure, materialism, family distinction, and many other ways.

2. Imagining we are saved by works is the greatest and most dangerous error because (1) it is the natural tendency of all people; and (2) it denies Christ's sacrificial, saving work. Christians, too, fall prey through attitudes of self-satisfaction and self-reliance.

3. God's righteousness is made known through the saving death of Jesus Christ, the atoning sacrifice for humankind's rebellion and disobedience toward God. This righteousness, given by God is a gift, comes to us through faith; it is "by grace alone, through faith alone." To receive God's forgiveness and salvation through faith alone is to exclude any and all effort and merit. We have no right and no reason to boast before God.

4. To be justified means to have a new start in life every day. God's grace is a forgiving, empowering grace that enables His people to live in forgiveness toward one another, to live with confidence and hope in the future He has planned for His children, and to be effective witnesses and servants in the world.

5. To assert, "You must give up . . .," is to place conditions on God's free mercy in Jesus; it is to turn faith into a work, and grace into merit. To be a Christian means to trust Jesus for full and complete salvation. To follow Christ means to respond to His love and forgiveness in His strength, as He empowers His disciples through Word and sacrament.

The Means of Grace (Article 5)

1. Answers will vary, but may include the way people have access to private entertainment and recreation, private work schedules and opportunities, and private lives in increasingly impersonal neighborhoods and communities. In a religious context, "bowling alone" may include the growing availability of television and radio worship services, as well as the popularity of para-church organizations and ministries.

2. Words, water, bread, and wine can seem so "ordinary" to some people. Many people seek miraculous signs, demonstrations of power or persuasive wisdom (see 1 Corinthians 1:22). The ministry of Word and sacrament is rooted in a "theology of the cross," that is, the central place of Jesus' death for sinful human beings in God's work of salvation. It is easy and tempting to "look within" for some assurance that we are saved, or that we are truly Christian. The Scriptures point us to Christ and His love revealed in His death and resurrection.

3. St. Paul teaches that the Spirit of God works through the means of grace—Word and sacrament—to distribute His gifts to Christians for serving the body of Christ and the world. In mercy, God gives many spir-

itual gifts to His people, but each gift is given because of His grace in Christ and for the collective good of the congregation and the Christian church as a whole.

4. The Pastor's ministry is public—a ministry of Word and sacrament on behalf of the congregation. The office he fills is instituted by Christ. Though Christians share in and support the public ministry, they serve Christ and the world in their regular callings (e.g., as mechanic, homemaker, attorney, etc.).

5. God nurtures and strengthens our faith as Christians gather together to hear His Word, to celebrate His gifts of forgiveness and life in Baptism and the Lord's Supper, and to support one another in our fellowship in Christ.

The New Obedience (Article 6)

1. The "New Obedience" is the life of the Christian, under the forgiveness and strength of Christ, empowered by the Spirit as He keeps God's people in the faith through the Word and sacraments. Christians may be reluctant to talk about "faith and good works" because it seems to draw attention to themselves, or perhaps simply because of confusion and uncertainty about God's will for living as believers.

2. God declares us righteous in the sacrifice of Christ. His mercy comes to us from the outside, with no contribution on our part at all. God "begins to make us righteous" as the Holy Spirit works in us to conform us to Christ and to bring forth the fruit of faith in our thoughts, words and actions.

3. For example, Jesus is the vine; only connected to Him through faith will we bear fruit. The Father and the Son together cultivate our lives as believers; we are daily nourished through God's Word and gifts in Baptism and the Lord's Supper. Many other applications are possible from the Lord's words in John 15.

4. Answers will vary, but may include assurance of His presence, confidence in His forgiveness for the many times we sin, the promise of His strength to overcome fears, temptations and moments of doubt, as well as His loving protection when we feel overwhelmed by circumstances. Christ's Word and sacrament renews and empowers us individually to serve Him.

5. Congregation fellowship, our unity and partnership in the Gospel, is brought into existence by the Lord Jesus. The Good News and sacraments nurture us as Christ's body, His people, whom He calls to witness to His love.

The Holy Christian Church (Articles 7 and 8)

1. Ideas about the church have changed as American society has changed in the past 25 years. For many people the church is no longer a central part of life. Attendance at worship and involvement in congregational ministry are static at best and declining at worst. Church educational programs and mission activities must often be accommodated to recreational and entertainment needs. At the same time, though, most people have high expectations of ministry, including quality worship, competent and accessible pastors and congregational staff, and modern and attractive facilities. Many other changing ideas and expectations could also be mentioned.

2. The church is "visible" in the local congregation where believers gather around Word and sacrament. The church is "invisible" in the billions of believers scattered around the world who confess Jesus as Lord and Savior and who have been redeemed by God's grace.

3. The unity of the Church is created and preserved by the Spirit of God as He works faith in people of all times and places: "one Lord, one faith, one baptism, one God and Father of all" (vv. 5–6). The Church's purpose is to carry out the Lord's commission to proclaim the Good News, to administer the means of grace through pastors and teachers, and to prepare God's people for serving the body of Christ and the world.

4. The dangers of compromise are that God's truth may be diminished or lost. The church cannot compromise on God's clear Word. The dangers of rigidity are that Christ's mission, carried out in the congregation's ministry, can be ineffective because of human rules, traditions, and opinions.

5. God promises that His church, the redeemed saints in Christ, will live forever with Him in heaven. Our Savior provides us with great comfort and assurance when the gates of hell threaten our lives and mission.

God's Work in Baptism (Article 9)

1. Answers will vary, but may include the joy at God's promise to bestow forgiveness, life and salvation to a precious child (the parents' first son or daughter) or an adult who came to faith after years of unbelief and troubled living.

2. Baptism brings Christ's work of salvation to us personally—one forgiven sinner at a time. In Jesus' death on Calvary, God declared all humankind "not guilty;" He fully reconciled the whole world to Himself. In Holy Baptism, God declares the individual "not guilty," and brings the full and complete work of salvation into his or her life. St. Paul's words in Romans 6 illustrate this truth: we are buried with Christ into His death and raised with Him to life eternal. Everything Christ has and earned for us He now gives us in Baptism.

3. To mention simply a few blessings, Christ roots us in Himself, He gives us strength and allows us to be thankful, and He teaches us God's eternal truth. The Lord Jesus takes away our sin, buries us into His death and raises us in His resurrection to the hope of eternal life. He seals us as His own beloved people in Baptism, just as circumcision was a sign and seal of the covenant God made with Israel. All the blessings God has promised in the past He now freely gives in Holy Baptism.

4. It is, perhaps, difficult to accept the "quiet, unassuming" truth of Baptism because most people look for striking displays of God's power and grandeur. Of course, many fail to recognize that the power of Baptism is dependent upon God's Word and promise. Through faith we receive forgiveness, life and salvation in Baptism, and through faith we understand Baptism as God's designated means of grace. Like the incarnation of Christ, Baptism shows us that God works in humble, ordinary ways to redeem His creation.

5. Answers will vary, but will include thanksgiving to God for His gracious gift of faith in Holy Baptism.

The Sacrament of the Altar (Article 10)

1. Answers will vary, but will likely include the assurance of God's forgiveness and peace after a particularly distressing time of life, or perhaps during a particularly joyful celebration of God's goodness in Christ. Christians receive God's comfort and strength as they commune, because they know Christ is truly present with them and promises His mercy and pardon to all who eat and drink in faith.

2. Christians have, regrettably, argued over the meaning of the Lord's testament, His promise, "This is my body . . . This is my blood." Many churches have failed to take Christ at His word, and to believe what He says. His gift remains true, though, despite the fact that His church is divided in its understanding of His Word.

3. St. Paul emphasizes the importance of the Lord's Supper by underscoring the Lord's own institution and command. It is Jesus' Supper; the teaching and practice of the apostolic churches is rooted in His Word. The Lord's Supper is His gift of His body and blood for believers to eat and drink. He gives it for the forgiveness of sins; and His people celebrate His gift in remembrance of their Lord and Savior. At every celebration the focus is on the Lord's death for the salvation of the world, proclaimed until He comes again in glory.

4. The benefits are, as Luther notes, forgiveness, life and salvation. These blessings are first and foremost "vertical," that is, from God to the believers. God's blessings also, however, unite the congregation in faith, and strengthen believers to live in forgiveness, abundant life and the hope of salvation with one another.

5. Answers will vary, but likely will focus upon the assurance of daily

forgiveness and the joy and partnership that Christians experience in together partaking of the Lord's Supper.

When Christians receive and understand God's great gift of forgiveness, they trust that God will richly supply every other need.

Confession and Absolution/Repentance (Articles 11 and 12)

1. Perhaps private confession is rare in our day because of a number of reasons: lack of understanding of its benefit, lack of time, misunderstandings, and uncertainty how to implement it in a congregation. Some people may be reluctant to confess their sins to pastors because of fear of rejection, fear of exposure, or fear of losing credibility or status in the Pastor's eyes.

2. The benefits include the Pastor's pledge to keep every confession absolutely confidential (except in cases of unlawful actions that a person plans or threatens to do in the future), and the Pastor's ability, through the Spirit's guidance and help, to apply the Law and the Gospel to a particular situation. Above all, the Pastor, as Christ's representative, speaks Christ's Word of full forgiveness. The Word of Absolution spoken by the Pastor is a certain as Christ's own voice.

3. David's psalm reflects the "rhythm" of confessing one's sins against God and then receiving His Word of forgiveness. No one can stand in God's presence—not even Israel's greatest king—apart from God's declaration and bestowal of forgiveness. Though we are God's redeemed people, "saints," we recognize that at the same time we are fallen children, "sinners." All Christians today live under the stain and ongoing power of sin—we still live in the body—and so live in a constant attitude of humility and repentance before God. We eagerly seek and hear His word of pardon.

4. In the same way, Christian worship begins with Confession and Absolution, as God's people, sinful human beings, enter His presence to hear once more His promise of forgiveness and peace. Confession and Absolution "sets the tone" for worship, as we acknowledge our need and receive God's gifts in Word and sacrament.

5. Answers will vary, but may revolve around the attitude of repentance and faith that the Spirit works in us as we live in Christ and are connected with His Word.

How To Use the Sacraments (Article 13)

1. The means of grace are God's gifts to His church. They are channels or instruments of His grace in Christ, using ordinary elements (words, water, bread and wine) to bring the fruit of Christ's atoning work into our

lives. As fallen children, we cannot earn or merit God's love; we can only receive it as a gift. Through these simple, tangible ways, God demonstrates His love by giving us the full blessing of forgiveness, life and salvation.

2. As Luther notes, the blessings are that Baptism "works forgiveness of sins, rescues from death and the devil, and gives eternal salvation to all who believe. . ." It is God's will that all people come to a knowledge of salvation. Since Baptism is a means to bestow salvation, the church is called to baptize all people—infants, children and adults.

3. Absolution is sometimes called a sacrament, although it does not have a visible element such as water, wine, or bread. It is, however, a means of grace, that is, through absolution God conveys His gift of forgiveness, as the pastor speaks the Gospel of life to repentant believers. Answers may vary on the comfort of absolution, but likely revolve around the personal assurance of Christ in the words spoken by the pastor.

4. Christians receive the Lord's body and blood worthily by believing His promise, "Given and shed for you for the forgiveness of sins."

5. Answers may vary, but will focus upon the way that God gives us assurance of His every blessing through the means of grace. Christ reveals His presence among us, and He gives His strength that we may continue to serve Him in our daily lives.

The Ministry (Article 14)

1. Answers will vary, but may include higher expectations of pastors as effective communicators, leadership in the church and in the community, counseling skills, and other professional talents and capabilities. Some points of conflict between pastors and congregations may be the specific directions of the ministry, traditions, finances, membership needs and problems, educational programs, worship, even personalities.

2. Pastors preach, absolve, and administer the sacraments in the church publicly as called and ordained ministers of the Gospel. The office of the public ministry is instituted by God, but God gives the Church, in particular, the local congregation, the right and duty to call qualified men for the pastoral ministry. To paraphrase Walther, the congregation possesses the keys, that is, the preaching and administration of the sacraments, but the pastor uses the keys publicly on behalf of the congregation.

3. The work (ministry) of the pastor is rooted in the ministry of the Chief Shepherd (or "Good Shepherd;" see John 10). It is a willing ministry, self-sacrificial, demonstrating deep concern for the flock. Pastors serve the Good Shepherd by serving His people; they act in His stead and by His instruction. They oversee the church not as lords—for there is only one Lord—but as servants. They act with His authority, and motivated by His example, strength and compassion.

4. Answers will vary, but will likely focus on the Gospel ministry that Pastor and members together carry out in their congregation and community. When both see themselves in a partnership, united in faith and trusting in God's promises, the work of the kingdom moves forward under the Lord's blessing.

5. Christians can support their pastor(s) by prayers, regular tithes and offerings, words of encouragement, and many other expressions of gratitude and partnership for the ministry of the Gospel in their midst.

A Place for Tradition (Article 15)

1. Tradition enriches congregational worship and life. It brings a sense of stability, identity, structure, a connection to God's people of different times and places, and continuity in the ways of Christian faith and life. Some traditions become a burden to the church, immobilizing a congregational ministry and draining people of their vitality and creativity.

2. Some human traditions mentioned in the Augsburg Confession include vows for religious orders, the observance of special days for fasting and rituals, and festival celebrations. At times, Christians impose human rules on themselves and others when they insist upon teachings and practices as binding that 1) are not clearly taught in the Scriptures, and 2) are not consistent with the freedom of the Gospel (e.g., specifying a certain type of congregational organization as "required").

3. Jesus' criticism of the religious leaders is that they elevate human traditions over God's revealed Word in Scripture. As a specific example, Jesus condemns any human teaching or practice that violates the intent of God's will revealed in His law (e.g., the Fourth Commandment). Human traditions can "nullify" God's Word when they presume to speak for God—when God has not spoken—and especially when they contradict the Gospel of full forgiveness and salvation in Christ.

4. Some details of Christian ministry may be adapted to local circumstances (e.g., languages, facilities, patterns of organization, schedules, etc.), as long as these do not disagree with or diminish God's Word and the truth of the Gospel. Nothing can ever be adapted if the integrity of the Gospel of Christ is challenged.

5. Answers will vary, but may focus upon worship, outreach ministry, or other Gospel-focused fellowship. Tradition often leads God's people into a deeper understanding of and appreciation for His Word.

Church and State (Article 16)

1. Some key issues include the right to speak out against abortion, homosexuality, or gambling; Christian Bible study groups meeting on the campuses of secular universities; prayer in public schools at graduation

services and sporting events; vouchers that allow parents to designate a portion of their taxes to pay for their children's tuition at a private school; clergy involvement in political issues; government prosecutors who bring charges of child neglect against parents for their refusal of medical treatment. These and many other issues are relevant in American society today.

2. The distinction is important because God uses different means to accomplish His will in the church and in the world. In the spiritual realm God's will is accomplished through the Word and the Sacraments. In the secular realm God's will is accomplished through reason and force. The Church must never resort to or rely upon reason and force to proclaim the kingdom of God.

3. Government is a tremendous blessing from God. He has instituted governments to keep evil in check so that there could be peace on earth. Therefore it is important to obey the government because it is God's instrument. The same principle holds true for all authority, parents, police officers, school teachers or employers. A nation that has no respect for authority is headed toward anarchy.

4. As important as authority is, Christians must remember that it is not wrong question authority. It is only God and His will, as it is revealed to us in the Holy Scriptures, that we accept unconditionally. All other authorities derive the legitimacy of their rule from God. The moment an authority requires us to do something that is contrary to God's will, it loses the legitimacy of its authority, and it must be disobeyed.

5. The church and its leaders must be careful about involvement in partisan politics because 1) it is not our first calling; 2) it is not our area of expertise; and 3) sincere and dedicated Christians can be divided on many political issues. The Bible does not speak directly to many modern partisan issues. The church must always speak with certainty of God's Word.

The Return of Christ (Article 17)

1. Many people today reject the possibility and simply assume that the world will continue forever. This is especially true for those who have accepted a cyclical view of history and the New Age teaching of reincarnation.

2. Many people today refuse to believe that Hell exists. For some Hell is just another way of referring to our present trials, disappointments, and sufferings. The notion of God's final judgment is easily rejected by those who reject the existence of God (who would judge), and by those who reject the existence of any moral absolutes (standards by which He would judge). It would also be rejected by those who have the unbiblical notion that God is nothing more than a gentle, sweet, grandfatherly type, who would surely not hurt any one.

3. What a great comfort it is to know, when we are separated from a loved one by death, that such a separation is only for a short time. A glorious reunion will one day take place, when we will be reunited with all the saints who have gone on to heaven before us. There before the throne of glory we will see our parents, and grandparents as well the saints of old. What great courage is ours in knowing that our greatest enemies sin, Satan, and death will not have the last word, but because of Christ, and the victory He won on our behalf, we are victorious! This victory remains ours forever, and no one can take it away from us.

4. Millennialism is the false belief that Christ's kingdom is "of this world" (contrary to His own words to Pilate; John 18:36). The attempt to make Jesus an earthly ruler is not new; He confronted this attitude after the feeding of the 5,000 (see John 6:15). Millennialism contradicts and threatens the Gospel because it fails to grasp the full meaning of Christ's work in its broadest, most profound sense—the salvation of sinners and the promise of life eternal in heaven.

5. Answers may vary, but the promise of Christ's return affects every aspect of the believer's life. As Christians await Jesus' return they will want to use relationships, work, priorities, and their stewardship that others might be drawn to Christ, know the love of God, and escape eternal condemnation.

Free Will (Article 18)

1. We enjoy many freedoms in our country today. The Bill of Rights guarantees such freedoms as the freedom to speak what we believe, to gather with those we choose, to bear arms, and to worship where we please. These freedoms are fundamental to our way of life in the United States today.

2. We have free will in other areas of life so it seems logical to many that we should have free will in spiritual matters as well.

3. Apart from God's grace we followed the ways of the world, we were dead in our transgressions, and objects of God's wrath. In God's grace everything has changed. We are forgiven. We now have strength to follow Christ. We have new life that lasts forever. We are constant recipients of God's gracious blessings.

4. The first part of the statement is correct. Christ has saved us by His death and resurrection. However, the second part of the statement is incorrect. It is *not* up to us to choose to believe in Him. (It's actually a good thing that it is not up to us; because of our sinful nature we would certainly reject faith and discipleship.) God's word is clear: We did not choose Him; our Savior God has chosen us. "For he chose us in Him before the creation of the world to be holy and blameless in His sight" (Ephesians 1:4).

5. Coming to faith in Christ is like being raised from the dead in at least two ways. In both cases new life is given; and in both cases the one who receives the new life receives it without any effort, work or merit. It is the free gift of God's grace. In other words believers had no more to do with coming to faith than Lazarus had anything to do with coming back to life. Christ raised Lazarus from the dead. It was an act of Christ's divine power and love. Likewise when a person becomes a Christian it is that same divine power and love at work. Since Christ is the resurrection and the life He has the power to raise the dead—both the physically dead and the spiritually dead.

The One Mediator (Article 21)

1. The primary role of a mediator is to resolve disagreements or differences through negotiation. Family counselors often serve as mediators, helping couples or parents and children to work peacefully toward resolution of conflict. In business, too, mediators help with negotiating contracts, work environment issues, and in many other critical points of dispute.

2. Some hold up their efforts or good intentions as "mediators" between themselves and God. Other traditions see the saints or Mary in mediator roles. Still other non-Christians see "holy persons" or religious practices as means to appease God or earn His favor. Only one mediator brings forgiveness, life and salvation: Jesus Christ.

3. The Law speaks of God's righteous character and nature; no human can stand in His presence. The majesty of God is simply overwhelming to sinful, mortal men and women. Apart from His mercy, we know only fear and the prospect of death. In the Gospel, however, God reveals His loving, gracious heart; He is our Savior God through the redeeming work of His Son, Jesus Christ. In Christ, we know forgiveness, joy, peace, life, and all the other blessings of salvation. Jesus is the "mediator of a new covenant" that is eternal and unchangeable. His death and resurrection are our assurance that we are children of the kind, compassionate heavenly Father.

4. Jesus prays for us always. His death constantly "pleads" for our eternal life and salvation. He stands with us, asking the heavenly Father to strengthen our faith through His Word and Sacrament. Answers will vary on the hope we have in times of hardship and personal loss, but may center upon the truth that Jesus is always with us, hearing us as we pray and praying for us, too.

5. Answers may vary, but will likely include our desire to share the Good News of forgiveness and reconciliation in concrete, personal ways with other people.